Stories That Shape Us

Stories That Shape Us

A Guide to Passing Down Wisdom, Love, and Joy to the Next Generation

PLUS a bonus chapter on
How to Discuss Controversial Issues with Friends and Family

STEVE MANN

ISBN: 979-8-89694-404-1 - Ebook

ISBN: 979-8-89694-405-8 - Paperback

Contents

CHAPTER 1

Introduction

"What have you learned during your time here on earth? And who will you pass these lessons on to? The wisdom you've obtained becomes even more valuable when you pass it on to a young adult in your life, be it a son or daughter, niece or nephew, granddaughter or grandson."

TOM RAPSAS

Picture your grandchild's eyes lighting up as you recount the day you chased adventure—or a nod of understanding when you share a mistake you'd rather forget. You've certainly made mistakes, faced hardships, done silly things, and had some regrets. But you've also shown kindness, sparked laughter, and perhaps had your fair share of danger mixed with excitement. You've pondered deeply, explored boldly, faced fear, expressed gratitude, and shown wisdom—sometimes all of this at once. You have learned to love and be loved, to give and forgive.

Throughout your journey, your experiences have taught you about life, and now you have values you'd like to pass on. How do you share these stories in a way that leaves something meaningful with the people you care most about? A powerful way is through stories.

At bedtime, my grandchildren would often say, "Grandpa, tell us some stories."

I started with classic children's books, but when I ran out, I turned to tales from my own life. To my surprise, they loved those even more. The following night, they would want to hear more stories, and I would share my personal stories—funny moments from childhood, and sometimes not-so-funny ones. They enjoyed these stories even more than the children's books.

"The books are OK, Grandpa," they'd say, "but we want to know more about you." Their words struck me. They didn't just want to hear stories; they wanted to connect to real experiences.

The stories didn't need big morals or fancy plots. Sometimes a simple, "One time, I was with my brother…" was enough to get us started. The kids didn't care about perfect endings; they just wanted to hear about real-life moments they could relate to.

As they grew older, I assumed their love for stories would fade, but it never did. The setting might change—around a campfire, over dinner, or during quiet one-on-one moments—but their hunger for stories remained constant.

And the stories evolved. The grandkids still enjoyed the same old stories, but as they matured, they craved more depth—tales that were thought-provoking, sometimes without happy endings, but with experiences they could learn from. Often, these stories sparked real discussions about challenging topics. I began to realize that by sharing my stories, I was passing on the values and lessons I had learned earlier in life.

My commitment to sharing personal stories with my kids began when our two youngest boys were ten. While helping me sort through old files, they came across photos of me shaking hands with presidents George H. W. Bush and Ronald Reagan. "How did this happen? Are these real?" they asked.

That moment made me realize how little I had shared with them—not just about my time working at the White House, but also about my upbringing, travels, and life experiences. They knew almost nothing about me!

Years later, while telling bedtime stories to my seven-year-old grandson, Benjamin, I mentioned how his uncles—our two youngest sons, both of whom are Black—had sometimes been followed home after school by the police or trailed in stores because of their skin color. "That's dumb! Why would they do that?" Benjamin asked, looking confused.

There wasn't an easy answer—especially for a seven-year-old—but it opened the door to more stories about his uncles and sparked a conversation about race and discrimination. Benjamin's curiosity didn't end there; the next day, the whole family joined in a broader discussion about bias and prejudice. That's when I realized how eager children are to explore values and beliefs—even the tough ones.

For me, stories are more than just entertainment. They're a way to start meaningful conversations and share my thoughts about the traits, principles, and actions that make life joyful and meaningful.

Today, storytelling has been overshadowed by technology—television, social media, smartphones, and an endless stream of online distractions. We hear how these advances are ruining our lives, but the truth is, they're here to stay. And while there's a negative side to it, they've also opened incredible opportunities to communicate, learn, and connect. Think of FaceTime calls with faraway family, or watching a granddaughter's piano recital a thousand miles away. The world's knowledge is now instantly available, and AI is making it even more accessible.

Yet, despite these marvels, technology has made it harder to pass wisdom and life lessons between generations in a deeper and more personal way. Many young people feel untethered, unsure of who they are or where they belong. This book hopes to bridge that gap through the timeless, heartfelt connection of storytelling.

My hope is that this book inspires you to use stories to pass on your own wisdom and experiences to the people you care about. In the process, you might just find a little inspiration of your own. The next chapter shows you how to unlock the full potential of this book by customizing it to fit your goals and spark deeper conversations.

CHAPTER 2

Using the Book Your Way

"We must all learn to adjust with our surroundings."

T-Pain

In writing this book, I experimented with different storytelling approaches with my own grandkids and encouraged friends to try it out. What I discovered was that they all had fun telling stories, but used the book in different ways depending on the ages and relationships they had.

In this chapter, you'll learn how to make the book yours, ensuring it becomes a powerful resource for achieving the impact you want in your relationships and conversations. Here are three approaches you can take to make the book your own:

1. **Just Enjoy the Stories:** You don't need to follow a strict order—just pick a story and enjoy! After reading, take a moment to reflect. What did it remind you of? What emotions did it spark? As you read, you'll get to know a bit about me

while having fun, and maybe—just maybe—the stories will spark some reflection on your own beliefs.

2. **Read with Someone You Care About:** For a deeper experience, read these stories with a child, grandchild, partner, or friend, then use the stories as a springboard for conversations about the traits, principles, and beliefs they teach. Just telling these stories to my wife sparked all kinds of thoughts and stories from her life, and the grandkids always have their own stories to share (be sure to ask). Telling stories opens the door to teaching and exploring important life lessons together.

3. **Create Your Own Legacy:** The most involved and rewarding approach is to use this book as a guide to identify the traits, principles, and beliefs that you cherish most. Then illustrate them through your own stories, sharing them with your grandchildren. You can use the activities and actions to explore the concepts in more depth. Write your stories on your computer, in a journal, or even record them with an audio device. This approach takes a little more time, but it's a powerful way to clarify your values and leave a meaningful legacy for future generations.

Tips:

- **Think of this as a workbook** where you read, share, discuss, and then—perhaps—engage in some activities that will help you and those you are reading with to learn more.

- **Don't force the process.** Have discussions when you feel it is appropriate, and choose to work on activities when it seems right.

- **You can read one story at a time** or read all the stories around a specific trait.

- **Take time to ponder** and reflect on what you are reading.

- **Don't rush.** Leave time for kids to think about the story and tell stories of their own. Be patient.

- **Adapt the book** to your own needs and the interests of those with whom you are sharing.

The next section gives more specific guidelines for various types of readers.

Practical Guidelines for Users

Parents:

Have you ever wanted to teach important life principles to your children but weren't sure where to start? This book provides a model for doing just that—with your children and grandchildren—while sparking meaningful conversations. Here's how you can make it work:

Find an Appropriate Time & Place: You can read the stories together at bedtime, while sitting around the family room, during a family meeting, or while camping out. These moments create a natural space for connection and discussion. Make it fun—no one wants to hear another lecture.

Dig Deeper: After telling a story and discussing it, explore with the kids whether they would like to learn more. If you detect some interest, use the questions in the "Possible Activities" sections to further expand each topic. Ask for their thoughts and feelings, encourage questions, and share your own ideas.

Adapt the Stories: Tailor the stories to fit the age group, but don't shy away from big topics—young children often understand more than you give them credit for. While teens may seem uninterested, they're usually paying closer attention than they let on.

Make it a Family Project: Use this book to inspire your parents or grandparents to document and share their own stories.

Tip: You might consider using some of the skills you learn in this book to talk with your children about current issues facing their age group, such as drugs, honesty, rules, morality, and drinking.

Grandparents:

Your children and grandchildren probably know little about you, despite your love for them. Most of them are eager to learn more about your life, and sharing your experiences can give them a deep sense of connection and belonging. Here's how to do it:

Find an Appropriate Time and Place: Again, just about any time will do—bedtime, mealtime, in the car, camping out, or sitting outside on a swing. Anywhere you find a little peace and quiet is fine.

Telling stories as a family

Write Your Own Stories: Use this book as inspiration to create your own collection of stories. Your grandkids will be fascinated by them. Start by listing the traits, principles, and beliefs that have brought you joy, then relate them through memorable moments from your life.

Go Virtual: If your grandchildren live far away, consider using Zoom or a similar application as a tool to connect. You can then tell stories and explore the values that matter to you.

Leave a Legacy: One day, a struggling great-grandchild might come across your stories and find the wisdom and encouragement they need to lay a strong foundation for their own life.

Have Fun: Tell your own stories—and invite the grandkids to tell theirs.

Grandmother Bonus: While this book is written from a grandfather's perspective, grandmothers undoubtedly have equally rich stories to tell, along with the traits, principles, and beliefs they have come to hold dear.

9

Youth:

As someone who still has most of your life ahead of you, you can use this book as a tool to explore the value systems that matter to you. Here's how to get started:

Reflect: Read the stories and take time to think about them—and the traits, principles, and beliefs they represent. What do these concepts mean to you? How do they shape and influence your life?

Start Conversations: Talk to your parents, grandparents, teachers, or friends about these ideas. Ask about their beliefs and the stories that shaped them.

Tell Your Own Stories: Think about experiences in your own life that relate to these principles.

Ponder and Discuss: Explore the parts of traits, principles, and beliefs you agree with—and even those you don't. Understanding the reasons behind your feelings can help you clarify your values.

Tip: Consider writing down your own thoughts and stories. You might discover new things about yourself along the way!

Couples:

This book isn't just for families with children—it's also a wonderful way for couples to connect and grow together. Imagine reminiscing about your first date or sharing an embarrassing moment. Your experiences shaped you, and the more you share each other's experiences, the more you will understand and appreciate one another. Here's how to use it:

Read and Share: Take turns reading the stories aloud. You'll learn more about each other as you explore the concepts together.

Discuss: Pick a trait, principle, or belief to focus on. Talk about what resonates with you, what you disagree with, and why. These conversations can deepen your understanding of each other's values.

Share Your Stories: Reflect on and share your own life experiences that relate to the concepts in the book. What moments shaped your values? What stories from your life could inspire or amuse each other?

Take Action: Decide on something you'd like to explore or improve together. Whether it's practicing gratitude or embracing change, these shared activities can strengthen your bond.

Tip: Let these discussions inspire new traditions or shared projects that bring you closer together.

Friends & Family:

It might be tempting to skip straight to Chapter 7, where we dive into talking with friends and family about controversial issues—and that is perfectly OK. But before you do, consider exploring at least some of the sections on traits, principles, and beliefs in the earlier chapters. These will help you clarify the values that matter most to you and build the skills to navigate tough conversations with understanding.

I hope you find my stories interesting and informative, but sharing your own stories makes the discussions far more meaningful and relatable. This next section shows you how to develop your own stories.

Developing Your Own Stories

This book includes seventy-five stories from my life. I have hundreds more—and so do you. Your stories can be funny, serious, long, short, or anything in between. Start with one, and you'll often find that memories of other stories come flashing back, revealing more details as you go. You may think your stories are unimportant, but they are what shaped you. Sharing them with others can help them put their own lives in perspective—and can be a lot of fun in the process.

Here are a few ways to spark your storytelling memories:

Recall Key Moments: Think of a time you learned a lesson the hard way. What happened? How did you feel about it then, and how do you feel about it now? Think back to your childhood, your school days, your first job, courtship and marriage, or adventures. What stands out? Write down those memories, and then think of stories around them. You can look at old pictures for inspiration.

Tie Stories to Values: Identify a trait, principle, or belief that's meaningful to you. Then ask yourself: Why is this important? It's possible that an event from your past made it so. What stories do you remember from these life events?

Chunk Your Life: Divide your life into segments—like your high school years, early career, a move to a new city, or parenthood—then write down the stories you remember from each of these periods.

The more you write and share your stories, the more detailed you'll become in telling them. Don't forget to adapt your storytelling to your audience—shorter and lighter for kids, more reflective for adults. Be sure to record your stories so they won't be lost.

Tip: Avoid the trap of thinking you haven't done anything important with your life or that you have nothing to say. Everyone has learned from their experiences—whether as a single mom, a waiter, an Uber driver, a teacher, an engineer, or a cashier in a convenience store, you've gained lessons that can benefit and enrich others. Just take a moment to reflect on your experiences, and the stories will come.

Your stories, like mine, can be entertaining on their own, but the real value comes from turning those stories into discussions about important topics that can change people's lives. Here are some ways to make that happen:

Moving from Stories to Discussion

Telling stories can certainly be done just for fun, but they can also serve as a powerful way to illustrate the values that matter most to you. As you can imagine, the stories in this book are not as detailed as when I'm telling them in person, yet it's important to stick to the truth. People— especially children—have a way of sensing what is real. If you're using the stories to demonstrate a trait or principle, honesty is the best policy.

Bridging the gap between storytelling and meaningful discussion is often as simple as asking, *"What did you think about this story?"*

In this book, I use stories to highlight traits, principles, and beliefs I value. Alongside the stories, I've included tools to help you think about and explore each trait or principle. You don't need to share all the information from these tools with your grandchildren (or anyone else); they're simply meant to guide you.

Here's a quick guide to how these tools work:

The Concept: This is a brief explanation of the trait, principle, or belief the stories are meant to illustrate.

Stories: These are stories from my life used to illustrate the concept, principle, or belief.

Questions to Reflect On: These are questions after each story that help you reflect on what the story is meant to illustrate, or help you get a conversation started. For example: "What did you think about this story?" or "Do you have a story like this to share?" These may also help you think of your own stories.

Key Point: After each trait, principle and belief, you will find a brief summary of why the concept matters. You might agree or disagree or have your own perspective—that's OK! This gives you a chance to discuss and reflect on your own views or the views of those you are sharing your story with.

Possible Activities: These are suggested activities you could use to help you explore the concept further. Whether it's a personal challenge, a family project, or a group effort, these activities are a great way to bond and learn. Hopefully you will soon develop your own lists of activities.

Actions to Take: This is where you can reflect on and write down the activities you want to pursue to develop your own understanding and application of the trait or principle. You don't have to explore or do anything, but if something in the *story* or *possible activities* has sparked an interest, it might be a worthwhile and fun endeavor. In any case, write down your thoughts so you don't forget. You can do these activities individually, as a group, or both.

Make It So! (Appendix #3): This explains how you can go beyond simply writing down an action you find interesting to actually turning that desired action into a reality.

Using the Appendix

In the appendix, there are four tools that can help you bring the ideas in this book to life. They are:

1. Morning Meditations

Over the last few years, morning meditations have become a powerful way for me to reflect on what truly matters in life. These quiet moments often bring forgotten memories to the surface, sometimes even inspiring new stories. In the appendix, I've provided a brief description of my approach to meditation. I hope it inspires you to take a few moments each day to focus on gratitude and explore what brings you joy.

2. Personal Thoughts on Equality

This is a talk I gave some 45 years ago on the steps of the Idaho State Capitol at the end of a march for equality. It was a cold, wet evening, but the message still reflects my views on equality and its importance in our lives today. I hope you enjoy it.

3. Make It So!

This section contains instructions and worksheets that can help you turn your desired actions into reality.

4. Website Materials

Here, you can find links to additional pictures, stories, and information, including the author's bio. You can also find the links to the bonus chapter "How to Talk With Friends and Family About Controversial Issues".

Now that you understand the tools to make this book your own, it's time to dive into the core of what truly matters: exploring the traits, principles, and beliefs that bring joy, meaning, and purpose to our lives.

CHAPTER 3

Seven Traits Worth Developing

"Every year I try to grow as a player and not get stuck in a rut. I try to improve my game in every way possible. But that trait is not something I've worked on; it's part of me."

LIONEL MESSI

Have you ever thought about the traits that have made your life truly meaningful? In this chapter, we'll use stories to explore seven traits that have brought joy and meaning to my life:

- Be In Awe Of Life.

- Embrace Serendipity And Change.

- Make A Contribution.

- Dream Dreams.

- Practice Gratitude.

- Look On The Bright Side.

- Take Action.

These traits are a starting point. As you read, you might identify other important traits of your own, such as honesty, hard work, or a good sense of humor, that you would like to share. Use the stories in the book and your own stories to engage with your grandchildren and spark discussions. Review the activities and choose actions that help you, your family, or your friends further develop these qualities.

Trait #1: Be in Awe of Life

The Concept

Life is a breathtaking blend of wonder and fragility. The older we get, the more we appreciate its beauty and impermanence. In the vastness of the universe, we are unique in our ability to perceive, reflect, and cherish what we see. Like you, I've had countless moments when life's wonder has stopped me in my tracks. Here are just a few:

Stories

Losing it at the Lunch Counter

The summer before my senior year in college, I worked at the Cattle Baron Restaurant in Jackson Hole, Wyoming. My friend from Jackson, John Bagley, could not stop raving about "Running the Lunch Counter." The Lunch Counter is a place south of Jackson Hole, where the Snake River is forced into a narrow canyon, creating powerful rapids. It earned its name from the whitewater rafters who often lose their lunch while navigating it.

John's plan was simple: wear life jackets, jump off a cliff upstream, and ride the rapids. He left out one small detail—this was a high-water year. The river was so treacherous that even professional rafting companies were postponing their trips.

Five of us piled into an old VW bus and drove 30 minutes south of Jackson Hole. We parked, strapped on our life jackets, hiked down the steep embankment to the river, and, without a second thought, followed John over the cliff into the icy water.

Immediately, my lungs felt paralyzed. I could breathe in but not out, and I began to panic. When the first wave hit, I went through it instead of over it, sucking in more water than air. I thought the river was out to kill me as it pulled me down over and over again.

Somehow, I survived. About a quarter mile downstream, I clawed my way to the shore, soaked and gasping for air. I didn't see any of my friends and thought some hadn't made it. Exhausted, I climbed back up the embankment to the bus, only to find everyone there—silent and stunned, but unharmed. No one said a word as we climbed into the bus and drove back to town, abandoning our plans for 10–15 more runs. Lying in the back of the van, I felt every vibration of the road and loved each one. I was alive, and that was enough.

Questions to Reflect On: *What personal experiences have taught you about the beauty, excitement, danger, and fragility of life? What are your stories of adventure?*

_____

_____

_____

Surrounded by Zebras and Wildebeests

My wife, Susan, and I took my parents to Africa on a safari trip. We drove south from Nairobi, down through Arusha, Tanzania, then back north to the Kenyan border, chasing the great migration. It was a long, dusty journey in a rattly van. By the time we reached the lodge, it was dark, and the power was out. Dinner was prepared by candlelight, and my mom—always particular about her hair—was understandably grumpy as she washed away the grime.

The rooms were built into *kopje* (massive rock outcrops) at different heights. The next morning, Mom opened her curtains to find a giraffe staring right at her, no more than ten feet away. From that moment on, the dust didn't matter, and the trip became her favorite.

But the best was yet to come. The following morning, we caught up with the migration and found ourselves surrounded by countless zebras, wildebeests, and antelope. The sound, the smell, the movement under the glorious African sun—all bound up in this ancient tradition of the migration. It was astounding, humbling, and awe-inspiring.

A herd of zebras on the Serengeti

Questions to Reflect On: *When have you found yourself awestruck by the beauty or power of life? What are your stories of being amazed by nature?*

_____

_____

_____

A Newborn on My Chest

The feeling of becoming a father for the first time is almost impossible to put into words. I'll never forget the night we took our first child home from the hospital. She was just one day old, and as she lay on my chest, I was overwhelmed.

"Wow," I thought, "here's this brand-new person—helpless, with her whole life ahead of her, and depending on me to keep her safe, help her grow, and teach her values that will not only bring her joy, but help her navigate through life."

I lay there, taking in the soft, velvety feel of her skin and that unmistakable smell of a newborn. In that moment, I don't think anything in the world felt more pure than the love I had for that tiny, perfect being.

Questions to Reflect On: *When have you felt a pure, unconditional love? What are your stories of finding humility and responsibility from the lives of others?*

_____

_____

_____

Frankfurter Platz from the Kaufhaus

My companion and I visited the market one Saturday morning (I was a young missionary in Germany then) and ended up on the third floor of the Kaufhaus—a large department store in the heart of Frankfurt. As I looked out the window, I saw hundreds of people bustling through the square below, busy with their weekend shopping.

I suddenly found myself struck by an overwhelming thought: "How is it possible that each of these people has hopes and dreams, fears and ambitions, struggles and joys, just like I do?" It was humbling to consider. Today, when I am in large crowds, I am often struck by the richness and complexity of human life.

Questions to Reflect On: What are your thoughts on the uniqueness of all the individual lives around you? What are your stories of experiencing the complexity of human life?

_____

_____

_____

Monuments of Civilization

I've been fortunate to explore some of the world's greatest achievements—both ancient and modern. From the pyramids of Egypt to the terraces of Machu Picchu, from the Roman walls in England to the breathtaking architecture of Notre Dame and the solemnity of the Lincoln Memorial, I'm continually awed by humanity's creativity and ingenuity and the herculean efforts made to pass their traditions and values on to the next generations.

One moment that stands out came during a family trip to Egypt with our four older children. We cruised down the Nile, stopping to explore various sites, including the Karnak temple complex. Inside one of the temples, we marveled at the vivid colors of the hieroglyphics, still brilliant after thousands of years. Somehow, those ancient artisans knew how to create paint that could last for millennia—while I have to repaint my front door every few years!

Moments like these remind me of the incredible legacy humanity leaves behind through art, intellect, effort, and invention. It also made me wonder what kind of legacy I could leave for my own grandchildren.

Questions to Reflect On: *What human creations or accomplishments have left you in awe? What are your stories of finding enlightenment through human creations?*

_____

_____

_____

Sailing with the Dolphins

It was a warm, sunny day off the coast of Belize, and we were at full sail in our little sloop. As we practiced turns, adjusting our course, and trimming the sails, someone pointed out a dolphin riding the bow wave on our port side. We all rushed forward to watch, only to realize another dolphin was mirroring it on the starboard side.

For the next 20 minutes, these beautiful sea creatures played alongside us—jumping, diving, and gliding effortlessly through the water. It felt like they were as curious about us as we were about them. When they finally veered off to continue their own adventures, we stayed silent for a moment, marveling at the beauty we had just encountered.

If only we could speak to dolphins!

Questions to Reflect On: *When have other species caused you to be in awe? What kinds of interactions with nature have you experienced?*

_____

_____

_____

Key Point

Life is a rare, fleeting, and precious gift to be cherished. There will be setbacks, challenges, and things that don't go as planned—but those too are part of the experience. The more we embrace life's beauty and fragility, the more joy we can find in the present moment. We need to take every opportunity to notice, feel, and celebrate the wonder of life.

Possible Activities to Further Experience an Awareness and Awe of Life

Try them if you would like, by yourself, with your family, or with a group:

- Engage your senses one at a time: notice what you see, hear, touch, taste, or smell more intentionally.

- Explore new places: parks, museums, zoos, concerts, lakes, or even a neighborhood you've never visited.

- Build connections, make a new friend, learn a skill, or volunteer to help someone in need.

- Hold a newborn—human or otherwise.

- Spend quiet time reflecting in nature or a peaceful space.

- Brighten someone's day with an act of kindness.

- Write down and share moments that have filled you with awe.

- Create a joy list: write down things that bring you happiness and look for ways to experience more of them.

- Brainstorm your own activities to cultivate a greater appreciation for life.

- Next time you go to work or on errands, try to be aware of the beauty around you.

Actions

To better embrace change, I will:

- Share the stories that have inspired in me a reverence for life.

- More fully experience and cultivate reverence for life by:

_____

_____

_____

Trait #2: Embrace Serendipity and Change

The Concept

Life can be smooth one moment, then suddenly change the next, thanks to a single phone call. Maybe you missed a flight, and in the same moment, you met someone who changed your life. Or perhaps you lost your job, and while trying to find your way, you bump into an opportunity you never imagined. Sometimes world-altering events, like the fall of the World Trade Towers, drastically alter our lives and our perspectives. Some changes are within our control, but many are not.

The key to joy isn't avoiding change—we can't—but learning how to respond, adapt, and deal with it. When we resist change, frustration often grows. It isn't the change that delivers or takes away joy, but how we react to it. Even unwelcome changes can sometimes lead to unexpected opportunities. Here are some examples from my life.

Stories

My Dad and the Onion Seed

When I was about ten, my dad decided to grow an experimental crop of onion seed. It was his first time trying it, and he was counting on the income to offset losses from other crops that year. The field looked incredible—rows of tall, elegant stalks crowned with flowers that held tiny black seeds that rattled when you shook them.

Then, the day before we planned to harvest, a sudden windstorm swept through. In just 15 minutes, the entire crop was destroyed. My dad, devastated by the destruction, came into the house and said calmly,

"Pack up. We're going to McCall for a few days." (McCall is a lakeside resort town about two hours from our farm.) And so, we went.

We returned on Sunday, and my dad, a longtime lay leader in our church, headed to his meetings as usual. At the church door, people greeted him and asked how he was doing. His response was always the same—"I couldn't be better." Later, I asked him, "Dad, how can you say that? We just lost the whole onion seed crop!"

He smiled and said, "As their counselor, I know their struggles, and, son, I wouldn't trade any of my problems for any of theirs."

That moment taught me a lesson I've carried ever since: adversity is all about perspective. Complaining doesn't fix anything; the best thing you can do is move forward and make the most of what comes next.

Questions to Reflect On: *How has unplanned change impacted your life? What are your stories of adapting to adversity?*

_____

_____

_____

Off to Zimbabwe

Shortly after one of my trips to Africa for humanitarian work, Susan and I attended a church meeting encouraging couples to go on missions. In the middle of the meeting, I turned to Susan and said, "We can't go on a mission with six dependent children, but what would you think about moving to Africa to help with the HIV/AIDS pandemic?" (At that time, HIV/AIDS was ravaging Southern Africa and terrifying the whole world.) Without hesitation, she whispered back, "Let's go!"

From that moment, we didn't second-guess a thing; we began preparing to go. The kids obviously had concerns but seemed to think it was just going to be a great adventure.

Five months later, we had sold our property and were living in Harare, Zimbabwe, with all six children. We left without fully considering challenges like schools, healthcare, or potential dangers, trusting we'd figure it out along the way. That quick decision shaped our lives profoundly, along with our children's futures and the lives of many Zimbabweans.

Questions to Reflect On: *What sudden, impactful decisions have changed the course of your life? What stories do you have of moving ahead on quick decisions?*

A Loss at the White House

A good friend, Steve Studdert, was working at the White House when he asked if I would like to join the White House Advance Staff as a volunteer during Gerald Ford's election campaign. I was living in Sunnyvale, California, at the time, happily working as an internal organizational behavior consultant at a semiconductor company—a dream job. But immediately, I said yes. I didn't know much about the role, but who could turn down such an opportunity? I told my boss what I wanted to do and, much to my surprise, he organized a leave of absence so I could head off to Washington. It was the start of a great adventure.

Six months later, we had lost the election. I boarded a plane in Columbus, Ohio, and headed home, exhausted, somewhat disappointed, and about 20 pounds lighter from the effort. I was so tired that the flight attendant had to wake me up in San Francisco to deboard.

What an incredible experience. Had we won the election, I probably would have moved permanently to Washington, D.C., and life would have taken a different course. Instead, I returned to California, joined two friends in starting a consulting company, met my wife, Susan, and was soon traveling the world. In that new life, I was learning new skills, building confidence in my abilities, and meeting the people who would shape the next twenty years of my life, engaged in humanitarian work.

Questions to Reflect On: *How have unexpected events changed the course of your life? What are your stories of adapting to change?*

_____

_____

_____

Boom Revelations

Once, after our children were grown, I overheard them discussing something they called "Boom Revelations." Curious, I asked what they meant. They laughed and said, "It's you, Dad!"

Apparently, "Boom Revelations" referred to the quick, life-changing decisions that seemed to define our family. Boom! We adopted two new babies. Boom! We packed up and moved to Zimbabwe. Boom! We headed off to South Africa.

I had never thought of these choices in that way, but the kids had spotted a recurring theme in our lives. They were identifying dozens of 'Booms'—some of them big, like moving across the world, and others small, like heading out for ice cream late at night. Some of these decisions were disruptive, but we regret very few of them. In hindsight, these decisive moments often shaped our lives for the better.

Questions to Reflect On*: When have you acted on a "Boom Revelation"? What are your stories of reacting to serendipitous events?*

_____

_____

_____

Train to Mombasa

One Christmas, I took my wife and two daughters on a humanitarian trip to Africa. Our group leader, filling in for the original trip organizer who had broken her arm, had never been to Africa before. When we arrived in Nairobi, we discovered that our connecting flight to Mombasa had been mistakenly booked for the wrong day. Due to it being a holiday, no other flights were available for the next four days.

The leader worried that we might have to cancel our plans entirely. Fortunately, I knew of a train connecting Nairobi to Mombasa. With only a couple of hours to spare, we scrambled the whole group from the airport to the train station across town and managed to secure tickets for the overnight train.

The group was uneasy about this unexpected twist, but the journey turned out to be magical. As the train chugged along, we opened the windows to the smells of Africa and the sounds of lions roaring in the distance, all beneath a brilliant moon.

On the night train to Mombasa

No one slept much, as we were too enthralled by the new sights and animal sounds. What could have been a tragic misadventure transformed into a once-in-a-lifetime experience.

Questions to Reflect On: *How have you turned a misadventure into an adventure? What stories can you tell of making the best of sudden, unexpected changes?*

_____

_____

_____

Key Point

Life is full of changes—some are welcome, while others can feel like a disaster. Unfortunately, sometimes we can be so weighed down by past regrets that we lose sight of today.

We can't change the past; however, we can choose how we respond to what happens now and in the future. Some people spend their entire lives worrying about missed opportunities or decisions they didn't make. Yet real joy comes when we embrace change, adapt, and look for ways to create something positive.

Possible Activities to Better Embrace Serendipity and Change

- Write down and share your personal stories of dealing with unexpected change.

- Make a list of sudden or even negative changes in your life that ultimately had great outcomes. Reflect on what made those outcomes positive.

- What is going on in your life now that you could turn into a positive?

- Is there something challenging in your life right now that you can turn into an opportunity?

- Write down and share a sudden change that made you angry or upset. How could you rewrite the ending?

- Do something unexpected—by yourself or with someone else—and embrace the adventure.

Actions

To help me expand my awe of life, I will:

- Share my stories of embracing change.

- More fully embrace change by:

_____

_____

_____

Trait #3: Make a Contribution

The Concept

Think of a time when you helped someone, no matter how small the gesture. Maybe you helped a neighbor with some repairs or cleanup, or maybe you stopped to see an old friend you knew was struggling. It felt good, didn't it? You are wired to make a difference—we all are. Whether it's helping someone in need, improving a community, or fixing something broken, contributing gives us purpose and joy. It's what defines us as humans and connects us to something bigger than ourselves.

Our contributions don't have to be grand gestures. Small acts done every day can ripple outward and change lives. Here are some of my stories about making a contribution. I hope they inspire you to reflect on your own.

Stories

Fertilizer Christmas

I'll never forget our first Christmas in Zimbabwe. Wanting to do something meaningful for the community, we asked around to find out what people in the rural areas needed most. The answer? Fertilizer. With a simple bag of fertilizer, they could grow enough maize to feed their families and share with others in the village.

Prepping the field for planting

It wasn't a traditional Christmas gift, but it felt right. The local agricultural representative helped us organize the event. We bought a truckload of fertilizer and drove up to one of the poorest villages in the area.

There we were, the week before Christmas, handing out bags of fertilizer. People were so grateful—even to the point of tears. To lighten the mood, our kids wore reindeer antlers with little jingling bells while we handed out the bags. The villagers laughed; they had no idea what the antlers symbolized but found them hilarious. Their gratitude and joy made it one of the most memorable Christmases of my life.

Questions to Reflect On: When have you contributed in ways that truly impacted others? What are your stories of making contributions?

_____

_____

_____

Boating Through the Ice Flow

Growing up on a farm in Idaho, our family attended church across the Snake River in Oregon. One winter, when it was unusually cold, the river froze, and soon chunks of ice started backing up against the bridge. Eventually, on a Saturday, the weight and pressure from the ice caused a total collapse.

We expected to take the long detour to the next bridge on Sunday morning, but community members got creative. They organized a fleet of motorboats to ferry people across the icy river. They had blankets and hot chocolate and were there to help us all get in and out of the boats. They had even arranged fleets of cars to take us from the boats to the church. I'll never forget that freezing morning as a young boy—riding in one of those boats, dodging the ice, and feeling the thrill of the adventure as I crossed the river to go to church.

That simple act of cooperation showed me how communities can pull together to solve problems in tough times.

Questions to Reflect On: Have you been part of a group effort that made a big difference? When have others made a difference in your life? What are your stories of stepping up during challenging times?

Working with Teens

When we moved from California back to Idaho, I was asked to mentor a group of teenage boys at my church. I was intimidated—mentoring teens wasn't within my comfort zone—but I decided to try.

I started by attending school events with each boy and taking them out for ice cream afterward, just to talk and listen. These encounters were sometimes awkward at first, but gradually I earned their trust. Soon, we were talking about struggles with schoolwork, arguments they were having with their parents, and even girl problems. They didn't expect—or even want—me to solve their problems; they just wanted someone to listen and understand.

I loved working with the youth so much that I was asked to develop some youth leadership academies. Soon, my friends and I were running several academies each summer, involving hundreds of young men.

In addition to the academies, we hiked and camped in the mountains all around the state. We attended all kinds of events, performed numerous acts of service, and explored life together. Once, we attended a live show of *Les Misérables*, and the boys were mesmerized. They had never been exposed to anything like that, and from then on, as we were driving to activities, they wanted to listen to the *Les Miz* soundtrack instead of the hard rock I usually had to endure. Hooray!

These opportunities have strengthened my own family, brought enormous joy, and undoubtedly made a positive difference for those young men. The joy of standing on a mountaintop, staring at the sparkling Milky Way with a group of young people who had never been out of the city, is amazing.

You don't have to start an academy to make a difference. You make a difference by raising a family, contributing at school, helping a neighbor in need with some groceries, or caring for elderly parents. You can contribute to your family, neighborhood, or state. You can volunteer with foundations, clubs, or political parties.

Questions to Reflect On: *What service have you given that unexpectedly changed your life? How have you mentored or guided someone? What are your stories of making a difference?*

_____

_____

_____

A Helping Hand in Rwanda

In 1994, a friend approached me about helping him deliver medicine to a hospital in Rwanda, which was reeling from a devastating genocide in which hundreds of thousands of people had been massacred due to their ethnicity. Neither of us had ever been to Rwanda, but my friend spoke French (the official language there), and I had experience in that part of Africa. So off we went.

We loaded a van with supplies in Kampala and drove across the mountains from Uganda into Rwanda—a spectacular drive. At each city along the way, there were hours-long, sometimes days-long, waits with hundreds of semitrucks carrying supplies headed to Kigali. Fortunately, we had acquired the right kinds of government permissions, and they would just wave us through. When we got to Kigali, it took some looking, but we finally found the hospital we were seeking.

There wasn't much destruction to the buildings and roads going into Kigali, but we couldn't help but ponder the atrocities that had taken place.

The first day at the hospital, we received a stark awakening. They were cleaning out a well on the hospital grounds and found dozens of bodies that had simply been thrown in. Next, we saw a line of more than thirty people—many with rags wrapped around their heads—waiting to see the one dentist. Most weren't there for dental care, but in the hope that the dentist could remove bullet fragments from their heads. These were sobering moments that deepened our appreciation for the peace we often took for granted.

Questions to Reflect On*: How have you made contributions to the lives of others? What are your stories of making a contribution when your actions might not have seemed logical?*

_____

_____

_____

Clearing the Lake

Our summer leadership academies for young men always included a service project. One summer, our assigned project from the Forest Service was to plant hundreds of trees and clear out brush to repair the shore of a lake. The sun was blazing that day, and the work was hard and heavy, but we pressed on.

After about five hours wading through mucky water, brush, and thorns, the boys had completed the task. They were sweaty, hot, and tired. As we made our way back to camp, I don't think I had ever seen them happier. They had done a great job, far exceeding the expectations of the Forest Service, and they knew it. That activity taught them more about leadership, service, and brotherhood than any lessons they could have listened to.

Questions to Reflect On: *How has working together with others changed your life? What are your stories of working together to make a difference?*

_____

_____

_____

Key Point

Self-worth and happiness are often discovered through contributions to humanity. No matter our age or health, we want to feel like we're adding value—to our family, our community, and even the world. Contributions can be as simple as lending a helping hand or as monumental as starting a movement.

Young people are often ignored or dismissed but can make huge contributions if given the opportunity. Older people, especially in our "modern" society, have high rates of depression and suicide, often because they are set aside and no longer feel useful. Finding ways to contribute, and helping others find ways to contribute, brings happiness and a sense of value.

We often marvel at the way people come together in times of catastrophe or danger to find solutions and make a contribution, but we don't have to wait for disasters to happen. We can make a contribution anytime.

Possible Activities for Make a Contribution

- Write down and share your stories of making a contribution.

- List all the things you already do to benefit others—you might be surprised at how much you contribute.

- Make something for someone else, whether it's a home-cooked meal, a card, or a handmade gift.

- Spend time with a child or have a conversation with an older neighbor.

- Volunteer for a local foundation, youth program, or community project.

- Build something: a company, a new device, a foundation, or a new relationship.

- Examine what you could do as a family or couple to make a contribution.

Actions

To make meaningful contributions, I will:

- Share my stories of making a contribution.

- Help someone else make a contribution.

- Contribute to my family, community, country, or the world by:

_____

_____

_____

Trait #4: Dream Dreams

The Concept

Do you dream dreams that you shy away from and are afraid to talk about? The ability to dream and imagine sets us apart as uniquely human. Dreams feed our souls. They provide us with energy, direction, and purpose. They help us exercise faith and envision a better future. Without dreams, life would be little more than routine.

Dreams are powerful, but too often, we're afraid to share them, worried others will laugh at them or dismiss us. Don't let that stop you.

Without dreamers, we wouldn't have the medical devices that keep us alive and healthy. We wouldn't know of far-off galaxies. We wouldn't create new art. We wouldn't be able to counter threats to our existence. Throughout my life, I've chased many dreams—some crazy, some life-changing. Let me share a few that have shaped my journey.

Stories

American Week

The first dream I remember chasing was during my freshman summer break from college. I was irrigating fields on our family farm when I started imagining a week at Brigham Young University celebrating America. The project was all I could think about. The next day at lunch, I told my dad about it and asked if I could take some time off to drive to BYU and see if I could get others interested. Dad looked at me like I was crazy but said, "Go for it."

I drove seven hours to BYU, and in just a couple of days, I was able to pitch my idea to student officers and the dean of the Fine Arts Department. They loved it, and the seeds were sown. That very fall, the first "American Week" was born. It featured articles, art shows, music, and a packed evening at the Field House with Paul Harvey, the most famous radio broadcaster of the time.

The next morning, Paul Harvey opened his national broadcast by sharing his experience at BYU. With the support of a whole cast of folks, my dream had come to life, and it taught me that acting on a vision can lead to something far bigger than you ever imagined. American Week turned out far greater than I had imagined, but without following that first spark while irrigating, it wouldn't have happened at all.

Questions to Reflect On: What dreams have you followed, big or small? What are your stories of making a dream come true?

_____

_____

_____

AIDS in Africa

As a boy, I loved reading about Africa, especially the story of Dr. Albert Schweitzer and his medical missions. The dream of making a difference in Africa stuck with me. Years later, in 1999, my wife, our six children, and I moved to Zimbabwe to join the fight against HIV/AIDS.

We didn't have a formal invitation or a detailed plan—we simply went. Upon arrival, I attended every HIV/AIDS meeting I could find and eventually realized that educating young people about the dangers of AIDS and giving them solutions were the most impactful contributions we could make.

My good friend and partner, Reg Nield, a Zimbabwean, started introducing me to government officials, and soon we were working with the ministers of health and education to develop an approach. We were stopped at times by lack of funding, uncooperative government ministers, or preachers who feared our interference, but we always found a way around the obstacles.

In the process, we came across a foundation called Mashambanzou, run by some marvelous Irish Catholic sisters. Together with them and help from numerous NGOs and USAID, we developed a program that eventually reached thousands of students, saving countless lives.

Opening the new HIV/AIDS center at Parirenyatwa Hospital in Harare

The development and implementation of the program united schools, religious organizations, and government agencies and eventually expanded to much of Southern Africa. It didn't start with a detailed plan, but with a dream and a willingness to do a lot of work.

Questions to Reflect On*: What dreams have you nurtured and pursued? Where have they led you? What stories can you share about following your dreams?*

_____

_____

_____

Learning to Sail

Idaho is known for potatoes, not for sailboats. But despite growing up in this desert, I was fascinated by the ocean and couldn't shake the dream of becoming a sailor. I devoured books about sailing, and eventually took some basic sailing lessons in California, where I met friends who first took me sailing in the Virgin Islands.

After moving back to Idaho, the dream remained strong, so I looked up weeklong live-aboard sailing schools where I could learn the fundamentals. I found one in Florida that seemed to fit the bill. When I showed the pamphlets to some of my friends, they wanted to go, too.

We spent the week in Florida with our captain, learning to sail and taking all the tests for a basic skipper's license. We learned how to navigate, make repairs, prepare, and sail just for the fun of it.

With little experience but boundless enthusiasm, we soon began chartering boats around North and Central America and taking our families with us. These adventures became cherished experiences.

When we went with our wives, it was usually two to three hours of sailing, followed by anchoring and going ashore for shopping and dinner. When it was a guys' trip, we would often sail six to eight hours a day—practicing our skills, but really, just for the sheer joy of being on the water.

Recently, I had the opportunity to teach some of my grandchildren to sail, and soon afterward, their parents went off to Croatia to get their own sailing licenses—all from what some people might view as a crazy dream.

Questions to Reflect On: *What dreams have you pursued despite them seeming improbable? How have dreams brought you joy? What have you ignored but could pick up and follow now?*

_____

_____

_____

Career Switch

Our consulting company in the San Francisco Bay Area was transitioning from local consulting to the development of management training programs. Early in the process, one of my partners turned to me and said, "I think you would be good at sales and marketing." I had no training or experience in either field, but I decided to take the leap.

I soon traveled the country building the national sales and marketing organization. Later, I began traveling the world to build the international division. The company became remarkably successful, and it gave me the confidence, connections, and finances to pursue other dreams.

By taking on something I knew little about, I was able to meet amazing people and have experiences that shaped much of my future life. Sometimes the dreams you don't even think possible can open new opportunities—if you just give them a chance.

Questions to Reflect On*: Have you taken risks that turned out to be life-changing? What are your stories of dreaming big or taking a chance?*

_____

_____

_____

Tough Mudder

A Tough Mudder is a grueling experience drawn from British military training. It is designed to test strength, skill, and endurance. The courses are held in various places around the world, and for whatever reason, I decided it was something I wanted to do—and convinced my best friend Delray Maughan, our son Parker, our daughter Torry, and her husband Chris to run it with me.

The event I chose was held in the scorching summer heat of the desolate Nevada desert, about two hours west of Las Vegas. The course included a 12-mile run through hilly, dirty terrain filled mostly with rough brush, a few cacti, and a lot of cowpies.

There were about ten obstacles along the way, including a dive into an ice-covered pond, a crawl through an underground tunnel, a swim with electrical shock wires hanging down, wading through waist-deep mud, and several climbing challenges. Some of the obstacles required the help of others to complete. While it was demanding, our goal wasn't to come in first but to have fun and help each other finish the course.

Delray and I were both 65, and we knew right away we might be in trouble when a young man came up to us at registration and asked how old we were. When we said 65, he simply said, "Wow! Amazing to see you here," and walked off shaking his head.

The event began in a holding pen with about 50 people, where they played loud music and worked to hype you up until it was time for your group to start. While in the holding pen, they began asking different age groups to raise their hands. When they got to the 40s, there were only a few hands. There were no hands for the 50s, and just Delray and me for the 60s. They cheered us on, but I suspect they were mostly concerned about our survival.

About six miles and several obstacles in, already covered with mud, we were starting the tunnel crawl when I heard a guy yell at his friend, "Hurry up, John! Those old guys are getting ahead of you!" (We later came across John throwing up by the side of the trail.) At the end of the event, we were exhausted, filthy, and stiff, but thrilled we had completed the course—and in relatively good condition!

Not sure I would do it again, but it was great to see my dreams come to pass.

Questions to Reflect On: *How has dreaming changed what you pursue in life? How have dreams brought you joy? What are your stories of dreams about adventures?*

_____

_____

_____

Key Point

Dreams are more than wishful thinking—they're what move us forward. Dreaming invites us to see possibilities others might miss. We have the capacity to imagine things that don't exist. It's why we have a space station and a Hubble Space Telescope. It's why we have great art, music, pacemakers, and vaccines. You might not fully achieve every dream you dream, but simply taking actions toward achieving it will bring joy. If you have a dream, you will see opportunities that others don't see. Working toward your dream will bring progress, adventure, and fulfillment.

Possible Activities to Better Pursue Your Dreams

- Write down your dreams—even the ones you don't share with anyone because you think they might consider you crazy.

- Stay in that early-morning state between dreaming and awakening to let your mind wander.

- Meditate regularly.

- Learn something new that expands your perspective or connects to a dream you've set aside.

- Talk to others about their dreams.

- Go to the mountains, beach, or somewhere away from the crowds, and think.

Actions

To further explore and pursue my dreams, I will:

- Share my dreams with others.

- Expand my capacity to dream and pursue my dreams by:

_____

_____

_____

Trait #5: Practice Gratitude

The Concept

I used to take simple things for granted—things like turning on a tap and getting clean water, or waking up without pain. But over time, I've learned that gratitude isn't just about recognizing life's big blessings; it's about noticing the small ones too. When we stop taking life's blessings for granted—whether it's good health, clean water, or meaningful relationships—we unlock a deeper sense of happiness and fulfillment. Having and expressing gratitude for people, experiences, and life's blessings brings daily joy and greater insight.

Babies are naturally self-centered, and as adults, we invest in helping them learn to look outwards so they can become contributing members of society. Perhaps the process of learning to look outwards is a lifelong mission. As we grow in understanding and empathy, we gain perspective and become more whole. Here are some moments that have taught me gratitude. Hopefully, they will inspire you to reflect on your own.

Stories

The Disgruntled Flyer

When I was traveling frequently between Boise, Idaho, and Harare, Zimbabwe, the journey often felt grueling. Sixteen hours of flight time, and nearly 24 hours of total travel time, made for long, exhausting trips.

One night, staring out the window seat at the vast ocean beneath me, I found myself irritated at how long it was taking and how uncomfortable I had become. Then I realized that just 70 years earlier, this same journey would have taken months by train and ship. In comparison, I was crossing oceans and continents in a single day.

That perspective shift turned my frustration into gratitude. I marveled at how far human ingenuity had brought us and how much easier travel had become. We aren't quite at *Star Trek*'s "Beam me up, Scotty!" yet, but we have come a long way, and I am grateful for the dreamers and builders who have "made it so!"

Questions to Reflect On: *What conveniences or innovations in your life are you grateful for? Have you caught yourself complaining about something you later appreciated? What are your stories of turning a frustrating situation into gratitude?*

_____

_____

_____

Exhausted at Zion's West Rim

Recently, I hiked the West Rim of Zion National Park with our two daughters and daughter-in-law. At 75 years old, I thought I was in decent shape, but the trail proved steeper and harder than I anticipated. As the girls chatted and enjoyed the hike, I found myself struggling and frustrated that I was slowing them down. I made it to the end, but it wasn't fun.

Hiking the west rim at Zions National Park

A few days later, I had my annual checkup with my cardiologist and mentioned how difficult the hike had been. He said, "I think I can fix that." Then, in just a few seconds, he adjusted my pacemaker, and overnight, I felt like a new person. It turned out the pacemaker was not allowing my heart to beat fast enough to accommodate the physical exercise.

Although I wished I'd had that "tune-up" before the hike, I was deeply grateful for the time with the girls and for the chance to look forward to many more adventures in the future. Gratitude helped me focus on the experience, not the struggle.

Questions to Reflect On*: What challenges—physical, emotional, or mental—have helped you find gratitude? What are your stories of being grateful instead of angry?*

_____

_____

_____

Morning Meditations

A few years ago, I attended a business retreat where our mornings began with meditation and breathing exercises. I had never tried meditation before and was skeptical—but I decided to participate.

Much to my surprise, I enjoyed it. Those quiet moments helped me reflect on what I was grateful for—my family, meaningful work, health, and the simple joys of life. When I got home, I began starting each day with a short meditation. It became a practice that not only centered me but also helped me approach each day with a more positive outlook.

In Appendix #1, I have outlined how I do this meditation and some of the things that come to mind as I ponder. I would encourage you to give it a try.

Questions to Reflect On: *What small practices or habits help you cultivate gratitude? What are your stories of finding appreciation in everyday life?*

_____

_____

_____

Watching My Heart Valves Flip

One day, I was mountain biking on Bear Claw Poppy, a trail in the desert south of St. George, when suddenly, I felt like I was losing my breath. I asked my friends if we could take a short break, as I was uncharacteristically tired and struggling to breathe. One of these friends was a doctor. He came over and started taking my pulse while I was resting. He said, "Steve, you are dying. Your heart is only beating about 30 beats per minute and skipping some of those. We need to call a helicopter and get you to a hospital immediately." I, of course, was too stubborn and was starting to feel better, so we rode our bikes back to where we had left the vehicles.

The next day, I called a cardiologist, and they outfitted me with a monitor designed to check for irregularities. I was supposed to wear it for a month, but the very next day, the doctor called and said, "We need to get you in here for a pacemaker." I said, "You want me to make an appointment?" He replied, "No, I want you in here now!" The next day, they installed a pacemaker.

Regular checkups on the pacemaker include sonograms, which allow the doctor to see my heart in action. If you ask, they will let you view the monitor. It is an amazing experience watching these tiny valves tirelessly flip open and closed. They do it some 30 million times each year, every year, without a single conscious command from me. It's a miracle of biology, and a reason to appreciate the intricate systems that sustain life.

I am grateful for my friend who noticed something was wrong, the doctors who acted quickly, and the technology that allows me to keep living and thriving.

Questions to Reflect On: *What aspects of your body or health have you learned to appreciate more deeply? What are your stories of finding gratitude in life's small miracles?*

_____

_____

_____

A Difference in Perspective

After several years living in Zimbabwe, my family moved back to the United States, and I found myself commuting every six weeks between Eagle, Idaho, where my family lived, and Harare, Zimbabwe, where I was still managing an HIV/AIDS prevention program. While in Zimbabwe, I would talk with people as they walked to work or to the market. I was often struck by the resilience and gratitude they showed. Despite staggering challenges—severe food shortages, hyperinflation, and the HIV/AIDS pandemic, which was killing thousands—they were smiling, laughing, and seemed to approach life with optimism.

Back in Idaho, I sometimes heard complaints about trivial inconveniences that, in contrast, seemed almost laughable. That stark contrast taught me to focus on what I had instead of what I lacked. Gratitude became a daily practice.

Questions to Reflect On: *Are there things you feel entitled to? What are the basics of life you take for granted? What are your stories of discovering gratitude where you didn't expect it?*

_____

_____

_____

Key Point

Learning to be grateful helps us find joy in the present and appreciate the people and things around us. It helps us navigate challenges with resilience and is part of what makes us more productive human beings. Losing—or never developing—our ability to be grateful limits our capacity for happiness and productivity.

Possible Activities to Better Understand and Express Gratitude

- Try a morning meditation to reflect on the things you are grateful for. These can be people, things, relationships, or anything at all.

- Make a list of the small things you take for granted, and spend time appreciating them.

- List the things you feel entitled to but perhaps should be grateful for.

- Contemplate how you think differently when you feel grateful rather than entitled.

- Read Morning Meditations Appendix #1.

Actions

To more fully appreciate life and the things around me, I will:

- Share my stories of being grateful.

- Enlarge my capacity for gratitude by:

_____

_____

_____

Trait #6: Look on the Bright Side

The Concept

Have you ever had a day where everything went wrong? Maybe you spilled grape juice on your new dress shirt, got stuck in traffic, and then received bad news at work. On days like this, it's easy to focus on frustration. But what if, instead, you saw it as a reminder to slow down, to laugh at the absurdity, or to find an unexpected silver lining?

The "glass half full or half empty" mindset reflects how we choose to view life. Life is full of changes, events, challenges, and experiences. When unplanned things happen—and they always do—some see them as scary and threatening, while others see them as an adventure and seek a way forward. Challenges are inevitable, but also an integral part of learning and growth.

This doesn't mean that we ignore problems, but rather that we focus on solutions. How do you feel when you are around negative or positive people? Wouldn't you want to give hope to people rather than crush it?

There are many terrible things in the world. The genocide in Rwanda killed some 700,000 people—mostly by machete—in just a few weeks. Human trafficking is horrendous; disease and hunger kill millions. But at the same time, productive lifespans are lengthening, famine is at an all-time low, and we have fewer wars, better health, and greater literacy. Looking on the bright side doesn't mean ignoring problems—it means choosing to focus on what's possible rather than what's lost.

With 24-hour news, we hear about every catastrophe in the world almost instantly, yet we are often blind to the good things that happen everywhere, every day. It's easy to get bogged down in the negative and miss the incredible positive stories all around us.

If we stay fixated on past mistakes, we become frozen in time. But if we can look forward, we might be the ones to make a significant contribution to health, peace, happiness, and the betterment of our own families and communities.

Most organized religions invoke the idea of repentance and change. While that may sometimes seem like a negative concept, repentance is essentially a way to let go of the past so you can focus on the future. When you get down on yourself, remember that you are better and more capable than you think. Here are a few stories that highlight the power of looking on the bright side.

Stories

Rock / Paper / Scissors

One summer I took our two oldest sons on a hiking trip in the Seven Devils Mountains in central Idaho. We arrived at the trailhead quite late, set up the tent in the dark, and tried to get some sleep. During the night, I could hear the boys starting to cough and get stuffed up.

Morning came, and it was obvious from their runny noses and hoarse voices that they had come down with something. We started the hike anyway, but after about a mile it became clear we would have to turn back. Not wanting the trip to feel like a failure, I came up with an idea. "At every intersection," I said, "we'll play rock, paper, scissors to decide which way to go."

The boys looked at me like I was crazy, but they played along. I remember the first intersection, with the boys looking at me, thinking, "Is he really going to do this?" Well, I did—and our random choices took us clear across Idaho, through some spectacular countryside, and into Montana, where we stayed the night.

Our adventure would have sent us north toward Glacier National Park, but when we looked at the maps, we discovered that if we headed south instead of north, we could take our time driving through Yellowstone National Park and then head further south to Huntsville, Utah, where we could surprise my wife at her family's cabin. Not having a key to the cabin, we camped outside that night and surprised everyone when they arrived the next morning.

Years later, my sons still laugh about the "Rock/Paper/Scissors Hike." What could have been a disappointing trip turned into an adventure to remember.

Questions to Reflect On: *What goofy things have you done lately? What are your stories of finding joy in unexpected ways?*

_____

_____

_____

Madadeni

As mission leaders in South Africa, my wife and I counseled and trained 195 young missionaries over three years. We also had the opportunity to work with some amazing older couples. We would take some of these senior missionaries, on assignment, up to the little township of Madadeni, about an hour and a half northwest of Durban, where some of the young missionaries were stationed.

To many Americans, the township initially seemed an eyesore, filled with rutted dirt roads, garbage, and mostly cinder block and plywood homes with tin roofs, often held down by old tires.

At first, I saw in Madadeni what many outsiders would see: the dirt, the dilapidated muddy roads, the makeshift houses. But as I spent time in the community, I began to see something else—children laughing, neighbors helping each other, the warmth of a place filled with life and love. I remember once arriving just after a rainstorm as the evening sun bathed the township. It was beautiful. I didn't see the garbage, dirt paths, and decay. I saw cared-for homes, children playing, and smoke coming from chimneys as families cooked their evening meals. It wasn't about the physical surroundings—it was about the vibrancy and love that filled the community.

Hailstones and ruined roofs in Madadeni

One time, a huge hailstorm hit Madadeni, ripping holes through the tin roofs and destroying dozens of homes and the meager possessions inside. The missionaries spent weeks helping people repair and rebuild. Every missionary who had ever worked there wanted to go back and help. The missionaries had changed their perspective. Instead of seeing challenges, they saw the resilience, tenacity, and love of the people.

Questions to Reflect On: *Where have you found beauty in an unlikely place? What are your stories of choosing to look on the bright side?*

_____

_____

_____

Almost Blind

As a boy, I didn't know I had terrible eyesight. I thought everyone saw blurry shapes and colors instead of clear details. It wasn't until a sixth-grade eye test that they discovered I was close to being legally blind. I used to carry around a BB gun but could barely see a bird, let alone shoot one. I didn't realize we lived in a valley surrounded by mountains. I was almost always the last one picked to be on a team because I couldn't see the ball unless it hit me. They asked me to umpire a baseball game once, and you can imagine how that worked out! But I was good at faking it. I would sit in the front row of the classroom and often got in trouble for walking up to the blackboard so I could see what was written.

Getting glasses for the first time was amazing. Trees had individual leaves, not just globs of green. Birds were real, and I could see what the teachers wrote on the boards.

There were hidden benefits to my poor vision. Since I was nearsighted, what I could do was read, and I did it voraciously. While I was still in elementary school, I read the whole set of encyclopedias cover to cover, all the volumes. I read Will and Ariel Durant's *Story of Civilization*. By middle school, I was into Churchill's *History of the English-Speaking Peoples* and *History of WWII*. I read biographies, philosophy, and the histories of other countries. I even tackled heavy histories such as *The Rise and Fall of the Third Reich*. Years later, all that reading made me wicked at *Trivial Pursuit*, but also paved my way to see and understand the world. I wouldn't trade it for anything.

Questions to Reflect On*: What obstacles have you or could you turn into benefits? What are your stories of seeing the bright side of setbacks?*

_____

_____

_____

Chicken Pox at Easter

As a boy, we would celebrate Easter by getting together with friends, having a big dinner, and then going to the park to hunt for hidden Easter eggs and roll them down a steep hill. I was looking forward to it, but just before Easter I caught chickenpox—so severely I was covered head to toe. Since chickenpox is highly contagious, I couldn't go to dinner, the park, or see my friends. I was devastated.

My mom, however, wasn't one to let a bad situation ruin the day. She stayed home with me, and we colored eggs. Then, to my amazement, she placed a table leaf at the top of the stairs and let me roll the eggs down the leaf and then on down the stairs, creating our own version of the Easter Egg Roll. You can imagine the mess as the eggs cracked all over the stairs, but Mom didn't care. It was one of the best Easters I can remember.

Questions to Reflect On: *How do you bring the bright side to others? What are your stories of turning difficulties into joys?*

_____

_____

_____

Steel Drums in Trinidad

One evening, while visiting Trinidad for business, my partner and I, along with our wives, stumbled upon a parade of steel drum bands practicing for Mardi Gras. There were dozens of floats, each surrounded by ten or so steel bands. It was loud, raucous, and fun. Before we knew it, we were swept up in the parade. Eventually, we ended up in a packed stadium filled with locals. It was pitch black, and we realized we were the only foreigners there.

We were a little nervous but decided to embrace the experience. The energy of the crowd and the music created a spectacular night.

Questions to Reflect On: *Have you ever found yourself in an unexpected situation where you chose to embrace the moment? What are your stories of making the best of the unfamiliar?*

Key Point

One can always find the negative in things, but one can also find the positive! Bobby Kennedy adapted a quote from George Bernard Shaw: "Some men see things as they are and ask, Why? I dream of things that never were and ask, Why not?" I love this quote.

Choosing to look on the bright side doesn't mean ignoring life's challenges—it means finding opportunities for growth, joy, and connection even in tough times. Optimism empowers us to move forward, inspires those around us, and transforms setbacks into stepping stones. It's not just a mindset; it's a way to create a life filled with hope, resilience, and possibility.

Possible Activities to Help Focus on the Bright Side
- Write down and share stories of looking on the bright side.

- List all the negatives you see, then list the corresponding positives.

- Reflect on times when someone's positivity lifted your spirits.

- Think about what you need to do to forgive yourself or others, and allow yourself to move forward.

- Read *Man's Search for Meaning* by Viktor Frankl.

- Do something goofy or unexpected just for fun.

- Read books or watch movies about inspiring people who overcame challenges.

- Make a deal with a friend to stop you every time you say something negative, and encourage you when you focus on the positive.

Actions

To better focus on the bright side, I will:

- Share my stories of looking on the bright side.

- Eliminate negative or damaging thoughts by:

- Bring positive energy to those around me by:

_____

_____

_____

Trait #7: Take Action

The Concept

Getting started is often the biggest obstacle to achieving your dreams. Fear of failure, uncertainty, or simply not knowing where to begin can keep us from moving forward. But action—no matter how small—sets things in motion.

We've all heard the saying about how to eat a whale: "One bite at a time." It's true. Even the smallest step propels us forward, while inaction keeps us stagnant.

Taking the first step often leads to new opportunities, insights, and progress. Yes, you'll make mistakes—but mistakes are part of the adventure. The biggest failure is not to try. If we try and fail, we learn how to do it better the next time. If we don't try, we learn nothing. Will it work out exactly the way you hope? Probably not. It may be better, or it may turn out differently—but just as good. Even a tiny step gets you closer to your dream, and getting closer allows you to see more opportunities. Don't let the fear of mistakes stop you from trying.

Here are some stories about the power of taking action.

Stories

Most People Who Climb Everest Go Outside

During graduate school, my professor, Gene Dalton, assigned us to write a self-reflection paper. Preparing to write the paper included taking intelligence tests, personality tests, interviewing people, outlining goals and fears, and, of course, engaging in self-reflection. In the paper, I mentioned that I would like to climb Mt. Everest, which caught Gene's attention.

When he read my paper, he asked, "Do you do a lot of climbing?"

"No," I replied.

"Well," he said, "do you spend a lot of time camping and hiking?"

"No," I admitted again.

He laughed and said, "Most people who climb Mt. Everest go outside." He went on to say that if I really wanted to climb Mt. Everest, I ought to get outside and start hanging around with people who climb.

His point was well taken. That summer I got a job in Jackson Hole, Wyoming, and learned to climb. Over the years, I've had the chance to teach family and friends the joys of climbing. While I never made it to Everest, climbing became a passion. I am seventy-six now and am teaching some of my grandchildren how to rappel. I think often of Gene's wisdom and have tried to follow his counsel. I am grateful for the kind and wise mentors throughout my life who have provided direction and perspective—and who have questioned and challenged me. I hope I can do the same for others.

Questions to Reflect On: What dreams and goals do you have that need just one small step to get started? What are your stories of taking action, even in small ways?

_____

_____

_____

Skiing on Impulse

When I was about fourteen years old, my parents went on a short vacation, and I was invited by friends to go skiing at Brundage Mountain, about a two-hour drive away. While there, I impulsively signed up for ten weekly ski lessons, forgetting that I didn't have a way to get there.

When I told my parents, they weren't angry—they took action. The following weekend, they drove me to Brundage, and, not being able to sit around the lodge, rented equipment and signed up for lessons. We left that day with a family annual pass to the resort.

The next week, I sold my saxophone for money to buy skis, and skiing quickly became our family sport. What began as a random decision turned into years of shared experiences on the slopes.

Questions to Reflect On: *Have you ever made an impulsive decision that led to something wonderful? What are your stories of taking actions that created new traditions?*

_____

_____

_____

High Hurdles (Not Every Quick Decision Works)

One day in grade school, they described the sport of hurdling, and I decided to try it. Having never seen a hurdle, I had to improvise by using the tailgate of my dad's pickup truck.

It was parked on the concrete driveway in front of our house, so I emptied the truck bed, climbed inside, and ran toward the tailgate, imagining myself gracefully leaping over it. Unfortunately, my toe caught the edge, and I crashed onto the driveway, cracking my pelvis. My mom paid the price by having to carry me around for the next several weeks, probably thinking, "How did I raise such a dummy?" The good news is that the story has entertained my whole family for sixty years.

Not every action will succeed, but every failure is an opportunity to learn. I learned pretty quickly that I was not a hurdler. Failure isn't the end of the road, but an opportunity to try something different.

Questions to Reflect On: *What actions have you taken that didn't go as planned, but taught you something valuable? What are your stories of learning through trial and error?*

_____

_____

_____

Zenger-Miller

Just out of college, I was in my first real job working for a semiconductor company in Sunnyvale, California. I was in the process of starting my own company with my boss when, out of the blue, two friends asked me to come to lunch. I knew they had started a company, but they were older and considerably more experienced than I was, so I was taken aback when they said, "We heard you were thinking of starting a company, and we are kind of disappointed because we wanted to ask you to join ours."

I was caught off guard getting such an invitation, as I didn't think they knew much about me. But I knew about them and the respect they had in the valley. It took only a moment for me to say yes.

Joining my friends in that consulting firm, Zenger-Miller, profoundly and permanently changed my life. I had great opportunities there, traveling the world and picking up new skills. The company became incredibly successful, and selling it years later gave me the financial freedom to spend much of my life doing humanitarian work around the world. It also led to personal milestones—one of those friends introduced me to my wife.

Sometimes, a quick decision can lead to a lifetime of unexpected blessings.

Questions to Reflect On: *What actions have you taken that have profoundly changed your life? What are your stories of seizing opportunities as they arose?*

_____

_____

_____

Surviving a Cyclone/Tsunami

I was in Cebu, Philippines, just days after a devastating cyclone and tsunami struck the nearby island of Tacloban. The destruction was overwhelming—entire neighborhoods were gone, and the airport had just reopened and was barely functioning.

*Stern of huge cargo ship thrown onto the ruined mainstreet
in Tacloban, Philippines after a tsunami*

Despite the chaos, we managed to reach Tacloban to check on students
and friends who had survived. There was only one mostly cleared road,
which had to detour around a massive ship that had been tossed into
the town. The city looked like it had been thrown into a mixer.

We were to meet with our friends at a church, which was one of the
few buildings left standing in that part of town. Somehow, word had
gotten out that we were coming, and twenty of our students were there,
even though they had lost everything—including, in some cases, family
members. I did not hear any complaints; rather, they were just trying
to figure out what they could do to restart and rebuild. What a lesson
in resilience.

On an interesting note, I learned that dozens of people had spent the night in the rafters of that same church trying to avoid the floodwaters. One woman even gave birth up there.

Questions to Reflect On: *How have you taken action in times of crisis or difficulty? What are your stories of moving forward despite challenges?*

_____

_____

_____

Key Point

Taking action is what separates dreaming from doing—it's about starting where you are, with what you have. Even the smallest step can create momentum, open doors, and lead to unexpected opportunities. Fear, lack of confidence, or not being clear about what we want often prevents us from doing anything, and that gets us nowhere. If no one took action to fulfill their dreams, there would be no cars, telephones, medical procedures, or space telescopes. It is actions that move us forward—both as individuals and as a society. Unless we act, we don't get an education, try a new sport, invest in a business, start a better job, or even engage in a new relationship.

Possible Activities That Can Help You Move Toward Action

- Write down and share your stories of taking action, even when it feels scary or uncertain.

- Reflect on times when taking action, even imperfectly, led to growth or success.

- Identify one small step you can take today toward a goal or dream you've been putting off.

- Encourage someone else to take a step toward their goals by sharing your experiences.

- Think of a fear or challenge holding you back and brainstorm ways to move forward.

- Get a picture or symbol of something that represents your dream and put it where you can see it every day.

Actions

To move powerfully and decisively forward, I will:

- Tell my stories of moving forward.

- Help others reach their dreams.

- Move closer to my dreams and goals by:

_____

_____

_____

Remember to use *Make It So!* (Appendix #3) to help you turn your desired actions into reality.

Traits shape who we are, but principles guide what we stand for. While traits help us navigate daily life with joy and purpose, principles serve as the foundation for the values we defend and the legacy we leave behind. In the next chapter, we'll explore four enduring principles that have the power to unite, inspire, and anchor us in an ever-changing world.

Four Principles Worth Defending

"The principles we live by, in business and in social life, are the most important part of happiness. We need to be careful, upon achieving happiness, not to lose the virtues which have produced it."

HARRY HARRISON

How have the principles you believe in shaped your life and the lives of those around you? The principles we live by—in business and social life—are the legacy we leave behind. They give meaning to our lives and guide us through challenges and victories alike. Helping children, grandchildren, and friends understand and appreciate guiding principles can help them understand and develop their own. This chapter explores four principles that are foundational for me:

- Freedom and Liberty

- Equality and Fairness

- Citizenship and Responsibility

- Peace

These aren't just philosophical ideas; I see them as the foundation of a healthy, functioning society. As you read, I encourage you to take time to reflect and explore. How do these principles line up with your own values? What other principles have been important to you that you would want to pass on to your children and grandchildren?

Principle #1: Freedom and Liberty

*"Freedom is the open window through which pours
the sunlight of the human spirit and human dignity."*

HERBERT HOOVER

The Concept

What would you do if your freedom were taken away tomorrow? For most of us, freedom is like the air we breathe. We don't even think about how important it is until it is threatened. Over time, history has shown that freedom is fragile, and preserving it requires vigilance, sacrifice, and action. We forget that our freedom to pursue "life, liberty, and happiness" is a rare gift. We are constantly debating, seeking, and redefining freedom, both as individuals and as a community. Consider these questions as you reflect on freedom:

- Are we truly free if we can speak freely but lack access to food, shelter, or medical care?

- Is freedom given to us by others, or does it come from the choices we make?

- Are we free if others around us are not free?

- Is freedom the ability to do anything we want, or is it more meaningful within boundaries?

  A professor once shared with me an analogy: "If you are playing tennis on top of the Empire State Building, you play much better tennis with a 10-foot wall around the court."

- What responsibilities come with freedom?

Stories

Checkpoint Charlie

I had the privilege of traveling to Berlin as part of the White House staff setting up a presidential visit for President Ronald Reagan. At the time, Berlin was divided between East and West by a formidable and ugly wall. The wall had become the world's symbol of the stark difference between an oppressive Stalinist state in the East and freedom, opportunity, and democracy in the West. More than 140 people had been shot or otherwise killed trying to escape the tyranny of East Germany to cross the wall into freedom.

President Ronald Reagan at Checkpoint Charlie in Berlin

The most famous crossing at the wall was called Checkpoint Charlie. I was fortunate to be there when President Reagan, during a dramatic visit to the checkpoint, looked up at the East German guards and then stepped across the dividing line into no-man's land. He looked up toward the East German guards and said, "Mr. Gorbachev (*then the president of the Soviet Union*), tear down this wall." It was an incredible moment. The Secret Service was nervous as the president stepped into East Germany, and the East German guards weren't sure what they should do. It was a poignant moment, reminding us that freedom is not guaranteed for any of us.

Some years later I was in Paris when I saw on the news videos of hundreds of people, from both East and West Berlin, tearing down the hated wall. Some were standing on the wall, waving flags and throwing down the stones. Many had tears in their eyes. I was so proud of them and wanted to stand with them. I tried to get a flight to Berlin to join them, but they were all totally booked.

Questions to Reflect On: *What do freedom and liberty mean to you? Have you experienced or witnessed situations where freedom was restricted or threatened? What are your stories of struggling for freedom?*

_____

_____

_____

Lessons from Corregidor

On a business trip to the Philippines, I decided to take a hydrofoil from Manila out to Corregidor. This small, rocky island south of Manila was the site of bloody battles: first, when the Japanese forced the Americans to leave, and later, when the Americans returned. While it is jungle terrain, reports indicated—and pictures show—that not a leaf was left on the trees due to the intense shelling. There were tens of thousands of casualties and countless deaths. It is now a memorial, a quiet, reverent place. While walking through the ruins of bombed-out barracks and tunnels, I found, inscribed on a stone monument, a poem by N.E. Graham that said:

"Sleep, My Sons. Your Duty Done…For Freedom's Light Has Come
Sleep in the Silent Depths of the Sea, or in Your Bed of Hallowed Sod
Until You Hear at Dawn the Low, Clear Reveille of God."

I wrote it down and carried it in my wallet for many years as a reminder that freedom demands both courage and a willingness to make personal sacrifices.

Questions to Reflect On*: Have you had to make sacrifices to gain or preserve your freedom? What are your stories of fighting for or appreciating freedom?*

_____

_____

_____

Drunken Prawns

On a business trip to Singapore, I was having dinner with a new representative I was recruiting. When I arrived at the restaurant, I found him looking at a copy of the *New York Times*, with tears in his eyes. I asked him what was wrong, and he pointed to the newspaper with headlines about crime, drugs, and burning cities in protest. He said, "What are you doing? Don't you realize that you (America) are our great hope to have freedom for ourselves?" I had heard the stories and read lots of history, but not until then did I realize that freedom isn't just about what happens within our own borders—it's also about the hope we inspire in others.

I told him that, in part due to its nature as a democracy, America was always at the forefront of everything new: medicine, economics, government, social issues, and technology. Often, these new ideas had unexpected consequences that took a while to work through. I then said, "Because we are a free country, we will work them through and come out stronger on the other side." I hoped I was right.

What about the prawns? My partner at this dinner ordered drunken prawns as a treat. I had no idea what that was. What a spectacle! First, they brought in a glass pot, then filled it with Chinese rice wine and dropped in the prawns. The prawns crawled around during dinner until they were fully inebriated. Unfortunately for the prawns, the waiter then opened the lid, threw in a match, and voila! Fried drunken prawns. The prawns don't really have much to do with the story, but they did make the night memorable. Perhaps it was just the symbolism—the unsuspecting prawns having a great time until—poof! They were gone.

Questions to Reflect On: What experiences have you had that remind you of the sacrifices others have made for your freedom? What are your stories of sudden awareness of your freedom?

_____

_____

_____

Robben Island

While in South Africa, Susan and I rode the ferry out to Robben Island, the infamous prison where Nelson Mandela spent 18 of his 27 years of incarceration. His crime? Fighting for freedom.

Our guide was a former political prisoner who had been jailed with Mandela during apartheid. As he described the harsh conditions—the relentless manual labor and the constant dehumanization—I was struck by the sheer resilience of those who endured it.

Mandela's tiny cell, with nothing but a mat on the floor and a bucket in the corner, seemed unbearably cruel. Yet, from this bleak place, he emerged as one of the greatest leaders in modern history.

The most humbling moment came when our guide spoke about the enduring spirit of hope among the prisoners. Despite their suffering, they found ways to educate each other, to debate, and to dream of a free South Africa.

When he was released and became president, instead of being bitter and seeking retribution, Mandela insisted on creating a country that was free for all, even for his oppressors. Mandela remained free even through brutal, long-term incarceration. Many thought that freedom and majority Black rule in South Africa would lead to a bloodbath; instead, it became a great study in the ability of one man to make a difference.

Questions to Reflect On*: How does Mandela's story of resilience and forgiveness inspire you? What are your stories of hope in the face of repression?*

_____

_____

_____

In the Shadow of Lincoln

On warm summer evenings in Washington, D.C., I would sometimes walk over and sit on the steps of the Lincoln Memorial near the giant statue of Abraham Lincoln. It is a peaceful place, even with the jostling crowds of summer tourists. I loved to look out across the Mall at the towering Washington Monument and the Capitol Building in the distance and let the feel of America's ideals wash over me.

I could imagine being there during the anti-war protests or the day Dr. King gave his "I Have a Dream" speech. I could look over at the names on the angled wall of the Vietnam Memorial and recognize their sacrifices. Inside, engraved on the stone wall, I could read Lincoln's second inaugural address, calling us to "bind up the nation's wounds." I could imagine Franklin Roosevelt encouraging a shocked nation with, "We have nothing to fear but fear itself." To me, this is a sacred, even holy, place to ponder the great American experience and the sacrifices of so many to make it possible.

Questions to Reflect On: *How have freedom and liberty (or the lack of them) shaped your life? What are your stories of gaining a greater understanding of freedom?*

_____

_____

_____

Key Point

True liberty balances the freedom to act, think, and speak with respect for the rights of others. It gives us the ability to dream and work toward those dreams. It unlocks our individual potential and the potential of our entire species. It brings joy and fulfillment, and it requires constant maintenance.

Possible Activities to Further Explore Freedom and Liberty

- Write down your feelings about liberty and freedom.

- Watch *Invictus*, a film about Nelson Mandela becoming president of South Africa.

- Write down three of your stories of experiencing liberty and freedom.

- Write down the areas where you feel bound: physical, mental, emotional, societal.

- Discuss what life without freedom would be like.

- Think about what you need to do to liberate yourself.

- Write down what you do that infringes on the freedom of others.

- Register and vote.

- Think about how you could eliminate barriers to your freedom.

- Read the preamble to the Declaration of Independence.

Actions

To better understand and promote liberty and freedom, I will:

- Share my stories of freedom and liberty.

- Help myself or someone else become more free by:

_____

_____

_____

Principle #2: Equality and Fairness

"We hold these truths to be self-evident, that all men are created equal, that they are endowed by their Creator with certain unalienable Rights, that among these are Life, Liberty and the pursuit of Happiness."

UNITED STATES DECLARATION OF INDEPENDENCE

The Concept

Imagine being judged not for who you are and what you are capable of, but for the pigmentation of your skin, your accent, or your religion. Unfortunately, for many of us, this is not hard to imagine. Throughout my travels, I have found that people share the same joys and hopes for their families as I do. They share the same dreams for the future and struggle with the same issues of food, shelter, education, and health. Now, imagine how much better the world would be if we could put aside the minor differences and focus on the things that unite us.

Yes, there are differences in dress, speech, and cuisine, but these are enriching and enlightening. Somehow, we let color, ethnicity, nationality, and religion become a threat and divide us. We seem to create differences even when they are not there. I don't know if it is some human need to place blame or put others down, but it stifles peace, prosperity, and invention for all of us.

As I interact with kids around the world, I see the same intelligence, creativity, and ambition with an enormous difference in opportunity. One baby dies of hunger while another goes on to get a PhD, not because one is somehow better or smarter, but because one had the opportunity to live a life free from hunger and war, and with access to healthcare, education, and safety. Think of what humanity could do if every child had that same opportunity.

Equality and fairness are not interchangeable. Equality aims to level the playing field, ensuring access to resources and opportunities without discrimination. Fairness, on the other hand, acknowledges that true equity often requires adapting to individual circumstances and addressing systemic barriers. Together, they form the foundation of a society where everyone has the chance to thrive. While we have made progress as a nation and as a world in both of these areas, we still have a long way to go, but the dream outlined in the Declaration of Independence is still achievable.

Stories

KKK & Police

We are a mixed-race family. Our four older children are white, and our youngest two are Black. I quickly learned how differently they can be treated. One son, while attending high school, was suddenly confronted by two boys wearing KKK hoods in the school hallway, who said, "We don't want your kind here." He once found a diagram of a lynching tree, penciled into his textbook, depicting him hanging from a noose. Even today, as grown men, our Black sons are stopped by police for no reason and followed in stores simply because of their color.

For those who haven't experienced this firsthand, imagine living in a world where simple acts—walking home, shopping, driving—are shadowed by suspicion.

Do I sometimes get angry when events like this happen? Yes! Like any father, I feel fear, anger, sadness, and incomprehension when my children are attacked, and sometimes I want to strike back. I often fall back on the counsel of a Black friend, who warned me, when the boys were little, "Steve, these things will happen and you can't fight everyone. Be careful with your anger." Wise counsel indeed, and I have tried to follow it as I have taught my children. I have tried to turn that anger into teaching and understanding.

Questions to Reflect On: What do equality and fairness mean to you? What are your stories of experiencing or observing discrimination?

_____

_____

_____

On the Steps of the Idaho State Capitol

One cold evening near Christmas, many years ago, I joined a march for equality that culminated on the steps of the Idaho State Capitol Building. I marched alongside people from all walks of life—young and old, Black, white, and brown, men and women—united in our desire for a fairer society. As we stood together in the frigid air, I was struck by the hope that fairness could prevail. At the end of the march, on the steps of the Capitol, I was asked to speak. Some 40 years later, I ran across that talk while going through some old files. It still does a pretty good job representing my thoughts on equality, so I have included it in the appendix. Unfortunately, the fight for equality is ongoing.

Questions to Reflect On: *What do you think of as you read this story and the talk? What are your thoughts on equality and fairness? What stories can you tell about inequality?*

_____

_____

_____

Native Americans Won't Talk to You

While living in St. George, Utah, my wife, Susan, and I were asked to pilot some innovative self-reliance courses on the Navajo Reservation in Arizona. It was about a three-hour drive around the back side of the Grand Canyon from St. George to Tuba City, on the reservation. We would go down every week to run classes.

I remember before we started, we were told over and over, "You probably won't get anyone to come to class, and if they do, they won't open up and say much, because you're white. And most of them will drop out after the first session." This was not our experience. The night of the first class, we had so many attendees that we had to divide the class into two separate groups. At the end of the twelve weeks, we had some of the highest completion rates ever. Not only that, but we also made great friends. We would go early to set up the class and nearly always had folks there just to talk about their families and daily life.

Tuba City is part Navajo and part Hopi, and the two don't always get along. At the graduation, someone asked, "How did you get the Navajo and Hopi to work together?" We didn't do anything. It's just that when people start to share issues in their lives, as they did in the classes, it doesn't take long to see that common interests far outweigh any differences.

Questions to Reflect On: What misunderstandings have you had about other races or cultures? What are your stories of involvement with other cultures?

_____

_____

_____

Mosque at Ladysmith

One Saturday, while serving as a mission leader in South Africa, I drove with six of the young missionaries who worked in the office up to Ladysmith, about a two-hour drive northwest of Durban. It was our preparation day, and we wanted to hike in the foothills of the Drakensberg Mountains.

After the hike, we drove into Ladysmith because I wanted to show them an extraordinary Soofie Mosque I had noticed on a previous trip. It was small, pure white, and incredibly ornate and beautiful. We were sitting in the van a little way from the mosque, dirty and sweaty from the hike, but full of admiration for the building.

Soofie Mosque in Ladysmith, South Africa

Suddenly, there was a knock on the car window. I rolled it down, and a young Muslim man asked if we would like to come inside. I said, "We would love to, but we're kind of dirty from a long hike." He replied, "That's OK, but I will need to ask you to wash your hands and remove your shoes as you come in." We were honored by the invitation.

He asked us to stand in the back while they finished their prayers. At the completion of the prayer, the whole group of worshipers came back and greeted us with smiles and warm handshakes. They explained to us that Jesus was one of their prophets, and how much we had in common as one of the three Abrahamic religions. They then invited us to join them whenever we would like. I remember hoping that we could be as warm and welcoming as they had been to us.

Questions to Reflect On: What are your thoughts about other religions? What are your stories of meeting with people of other faiths?

_____

_____

_____

Turkish Guest Workers

As a young missionary in Germany in the early '70s, we would knock on doors to talk with people about religion. It was the time of marches in Washington, DC, for equality and the fight for civil rights in the U.S. I will never forget knocking on a door and being greeted by a young man who, seeing we were American, immediately began to berate us for our treatment of Black Americans. I listened for a while and agreed we needed to do more. Not wanting to bring up the Holocaust, I simply asked how he could explain the horrible treatment of Turkish guest workers in Germany.

His reply was, "That's different. They aren't people—they are animals."

Seeing no possibility for rational discussion, I simply walked away. But to this day, I wonder where my own blind spots are when it comes to equality and fairness.

Questions to Reflect On: Where are your blind spots when it comes to equality and fairness? What are your stories of seeing or experiencing hate?

_____

_____

_____

Key Point

Equality and fairness mean creating a world where everyone has the opportunity to thrive, regardless of their background or circumstances. It's not just about treating everyone the same—it's about recognizing and addressing systemic barriers so that true equality can exist. When we embrace these principles, we foster trust, strengthen communities, and ensure that everyone has a voice and a chance to succeed.

Some personal questions we might ask as we explore freedom and equality are:

- "Is one equal if all are not equal?"

- "Can we utilize the talents and ambitions of everyone, not just those who think the way we do?"

- "Do we stand up for those who can't, because we can?"

- "Do we believe every child deserves the right to basic nutrition, healthcare, education, safety, and opportunity?"

Possible Activities to Better Understand and Advance Principles of Equality and Fairness

- Answer the questions under Key Point for yourself.

- Reflect on moments when you've experienced or witnessed unfairness. What did you learn?

- Write down your own feelings about equality.

- Examine your own beliefs about other cultures or people.

- Read the talk on equality (Appendix 2) and note your thoughts.

- Write down things you could do to remove barriers for others.

- Try to understand why others do what they do or believe what they believe.

- Study, write, vote, and participate.

- What other activities can you think of that would further your understanding of equality?

Actions

To better understand and promote the principles of equality and fairness, I will:

- Share my stories of acting for greater equality and fairness.

- Promote fairness and equality in my family and community by:

_____

_____

_____

Principle #3: Citizenship and Responsibility

"Diversity, independence, empathy and perspective are essential values of global citizenship."

Welsh Centre for International Affairs

The Concept

E pluribus unum, the traditional motto of the United States, appears on the Great Seal and other official emblems. Translated as "Out of many, one," it conveys the ideal that individuals, despite their differences, can unite to achieve shared goals like liberty, peace, safety, and prosperity. This idea applies at local, national, and global levels.

Over 450 years ago, Socrates observed, "We are not citizens of just our hometowns or nations, but of the world." Citizenship—whether of a country or the world—implies responsibility and stewardship. Each generation must fight to preserve freedom and liberty, addressing unique challenges like oppression, climate change, famine, or war. We all play a role in this ongoing struggle.

NOTE: I am writing this as an American citizen. While I hope you can learn from the American experience, those of you reading this from other countries should insert stories and principles drawn from your own experiences and history.

Stories

Marching for Freedom

Occasionally, I participate in discussions and public marches to highlight causes that I believe in. These moments allow me to exercise my rights as a citizen and speak out for justice.

In college, the Vietnam War dominated discussions. Later in life, my focus shifted to civil and human rights. I vividly recall joining a "Black Lives Matter" march on the Las Vegas Strip. At 70 I was one of the oldest participants, and among the few white attendees.

During the march, a young Black man approached me and said, "I just want you to how much it means to me that you are here with us. Thank you." His words reaffirmed the importance of solidarity and action.

Questions to Reflect On*: What experiences have you had that made you feel a responsibility for your country? What are your stories of standing up for what you believe?*

_____

_____

_____

Pledge of Allegiance

As a child in the small, unincorporated community of Apple Valley, Idaho, I would line up each morning in front of our two-story, red-brick old schoolhouse (it even had a belfry on top) to say the Pledge of

Allegiance. We stood there with our hands over our hearts, no matter what the weather, watching the flag being raised. At the time, I didn't think much of it, but in retrospect, that simple morning ceremony marked my early awareness of what it means to be an American.

Questions to Reflect On: *What early experiences made you aware of your citizenship? What are your stories of becoming a responsible citizen?*

_____

_____

_____

Speaking at the UN

While working on HIV/AIDS prevention, I was invited by the Zimbabwean government to be one of their representatives at the first United Nations Summit on HIV/AIDS. My role was to present our approach to educating schoolchildren on prevention.

I had followed the development of the United Nations since I was a child, and I was grateful to have the opportunity. Although the UN is often criticized for inefficiency or political bias, I saw it as a platform for nations to collaborate on global challenges like health, immigration, and climate change.

I was expecting just a few people, but as I set up for my presentation in a large conference room, I found, to my surprise, the room was nearly full. People from all over the world had come together to try to find a way to halt this horrible disease.

As our planet has become more crowded and the battle for resources more intense, we have, at the same time, become more interdependent. Like it or not, we are citizens of the world and must find ways to collaborate for our own survival.

Questions to Reflect On: How do you feel about being a citizen of the world? What are your stories of contributing to or collaborating to solve community problems?

_____

_____

_____

Sequoia on the Potomac

During the Ford administration, I was recruited by the White House to work as a volunteer member of the advance staff. That meant traveling to cities before a presidential visit to help set up the trip. My particular area was press advance. As part of the recruitment and training, they invited us to spend an evening on the Potomac River on the presidential yacht, the Sequoia. (Once in office, President Carter got rid of the Sequoia, viewing it as an extravagance.) For me, a young man from a potato farm in Idaho, with an obsession for sailing, it was a remarkable experience cruising up the Potomac on the 4th of July with fireworks going off around the Mall. While I was always proud to be an American, this was an especially poignant moment for me.

Presidential yacht the "Sequoia" in Washington D.C.

Questions to Reflect On: *What events of yours have triggered pride in your country or community? What are your stories of devotion to a group or cause?*

_____

_____

_____

Military on the Beach

After six years of deferments, I found myself in graduate school with a low draft number. To have some control over my future, I joined a local Army Reserve unit. Serving in the military was never in my plans, but it was a requirement and turned out to be a terrific experience.

It started with driving my car across the country to Fort Dix for basic training. I was in good shape, so I aced the PT test right from the start, and because I was in graduate school, they put me in their leadership academy. I made a great friend from Queens there, so most weekends we would go body surfing on the Jersey Shore, to his cabin in upstate New York, or get dates to go into the city.

On my return to Utah, I got a call from General McKeen, the commanding general of all the Army Reserve units in Utah and the six surrounding states, as well as a professor at the University of Utah. He noticed I was in grad school in the field of organizational behavior, and so for the next four years I worked for him doing research on recruitment. *Tough duty for a Spec 4!*

When I moved to California, General McKeen introduced me to a friend of his there, also a general, who arranged for me to join his unit just up the road from my work. They didn't have a job like the one I had in Utah, but they had an opening for a race relations specialist. So, at the next two-week summer camp, he sent me to Race Relations School in Monterey. They didn't have room in their barracks on base, so I "had" to stay in a hotel on the beach. That's where I spent my remaining two summer camps. What a great opportunity!

While serving in the military was not my first choice, I had wonderful experiences, learned a lot, made great friends, and left with a much greater respect for the military and those who serve. I learned that service is often about being a part of something bigger than yourself. That time in the military helped shape me for humanitarian service in Africa and around the world. I am grateful for the opportunity.

Questions to Reflect On: What are your thoughts about service in the military? What do you think about a national service requirement? What are your stories about military service?

_____

_____

_____

Key Point

Being a citizen—whether of a nation or the world—is about contributing to the well-being of our communities and society as a whole. America's democratic experiment is unique, striving to balance multicultural integration with technological and social change. It has never been done before. America is a proud country, and I am proud to be a part of it. It does great things, but like all countries, it sometimes struggles with the very ideals it claims to value most. It makes mistakes, but being a democratic nation, it eventually finds ways to right its wrongs. What an exciting place to live.

Similarly, global citizenship calls for appreciating cultural differences, learning from them, and working collaboratively to address universal challenges. In an increasingly crowded and interdependent world, we simply no longer have the option of total independence. As stewards of our planet and communities, we have a responsibility to support, strengthen, and uplift one another.

Possible Activities to Better Understand Citizenship and Responsibility

- Write down your feelings about being a citizen of the nation and the world.

- Read the Preamble to the Constitution.

- Read the United Nations Charter.

- Visit a military cemetery or monument in your area and write down your feelings.

- Register and vote or run for an elective office.

- Write to a congressperson or sign a petition.

- Identify what issues are most important to you.

- Join a group or participate in a protest.

- Discuss with others what America means to you.

- Discuss what being a citizen of the world means to you.

Actions

To become a more knowledgeable and responsible citizen, I will:

- Share my stories of citizenship with others.

- Promote citizenship and responsibility in my state, country, or the world by:

_____

_____

_____

Principle #4: Peace

*"We can never obtain peace in the outer world
until we make peace with ourselves."*

DALAI LAMA XIV

The Concept

Peace is a multilayered word with ever-evolving meanings. For parents of young children, it might mean the rare quiet moment late at night when everyone is fed and asleep. For others, peace may signify the absence of war or simply a state of mind. But peace isn't just the absence of turmoil—it is the result of proaction, of harmony-building, and of active peacemaking. It comes from justice and equality.

While we like to think of peace as normal, history shows us it is more fleeting than we would like to believe—both between and within countries.

Personal peace, too, is not automatic. Many philosophers and religious leaders suggest it begins within us. For some, peace comes through meditation or prayer; for others, it is the result of overcoming an internal struggle. Each person must find and maintain peace in their own way.

Stories

A Father's Apology

I had returned from serving a mission for my church, had been president of my sophomore class at university, and was working while attending school. One day I went skiing in Park City with my father and mother. On the way up the lift, Dad started arguing with me about my hair being too long. (*It wasn't.*) For whatever reason, this struck me badly, and I kind of exploded with anger, saying, "Look, I have done all these things you expected of me, and all you can do is criticize my hair." I was about to say things I would have lived to regret when, unexpectedly, my father turned to me and apologized. He said, "You're right. I'm proud of you, and I shouldn't just be focusing on little things I don't like."

In one moment, my very wise father turned what could have been a disastrous confrontation into a moment of love. He was a peacemaker, and I was the beneficiary.

Questions to Reflect On: *Have you seen a potentially disastrous confrontation defused by a peacemaker? What are your stories of helping to create peace?*

_____

_____

_____

A Scar on Her Head

While working in Zimbabwe on HIV/AIDS prevention, I often visited the African World Health Organization (WHO) offices. One day, while waiting for an appointment, I started talking to the receptionist, a woman from Liberia.

I commented that I didn't believe Zimbabwe could descend into the chaos seen in other African nations. She said, "Steve, come here and feel my head." Hesitantly, I did, and felt a long scar running from front to back along her scalp. She explained, "That is from a bullet. I didn't think such violence could happen in my country either, but within weeks rebels overran us. I saw my husband murdered and one of my children die of starvation. Don't ever think it can't happen to you." Her lesson was a sobering reminder to me that peace is not guaranteed.

Questions to Reflect On: *How do you experience peace? What are your stories about finding or developing peace?*

_____

_____

_____

High in the Tetons

I learned to climb in the Teton Mountain Range in Jackson, Wyoming. Sometimes the hike to the cliffs took hours, so we would leave before sunrise to reach our climbing area. We would set up to climb various pitches and start our ascent.

Jackson Hole is a spectacular place with soaring mountains, lush green valleys, and clear blue sky. After a long climb, I would often find myself—muscles finally relaxed—sitting on a block of solid granite, looking out across the valley with no sound or interruptions, just the warm sun shining on my face. There, in the quiet solitude of the space and the permanence of the granite, I would feel a tangible, almost indescribable peace and connection to the world.

Questions to Reflect On: *Where are the places, and what are the experiences, that bring you peace? What are your stories of finding or experiencing peace?*

_____

_____

_____

Empty Eyes and Kalashnikovs

Shortly after the Rwandan genocide, I was delivering medical supplies from Uganda into Kigali. At the entrance to each city, we encountered teenage soldiers armed with Kalashnikovs, checking the paperwork. I wasn't too bothered, as I had passed through many guarded checkpoints before. What was sobering was looking into their eyes and seeing such emptiness.

I realized these young men had witnessed—and perhaps participated in—the slaughter of over 700,000 people, mostly by machete, in recent months. The immense emotional and psychological scars were evident. Despite their pasts, many of them eventually rebuilt their lives and contributed to the rebuilding of society. At the time, I felt profound gratitude to live in a time and place of relative peace.

Young soldiers patrolling the city on the way to Kigali, Rwanda

Questions to Reflect On: *What experiences make you appreciate peace? What are your personal stories about peace? How can you bring peace to others?*

_____

_____

_____

Peace on a Plane

I did a lot of air travel in my younger days and would often find a somewhat strange sense of peace on long flights to Europe, Africa, or Asia. Traveling alone, with no kids to worry about, I could let my mind wander. Air travel was less chaotic then, and I could usually book a window seat where I could look down on the endless ocean lit only by the moon and the stars. It was a time with no distractions, when I could

117

read, ponder (uninterrupted), and review what was coming next. It was a time to reflect on life, religion, and love. It was a time to be grateful. There really was a sense of peace.

Questions to Reflect On: *How do you find peace? What are your stories of finding peace in unlikely places?*

_____

_____

_____

Key Point

Peace is more than the absence of conflict—it's the presence of harmony, understanding, and compassion in our relationships, our communities, and the world. It begins within us, through self-reflection and empathy, and grows outward as we work to bridge divides, resolve disagreements, and create environments where everyone feels safe and valued.

Possible Activities to Better Understand and Achieve Peace

- Reflect on what peace means to you.

- Find a favorite book or poem about peace.

- Visit a peace garden or Holocaust memorial and write down your thoughts.

- Identify individuals you would consider peacemakers and describe why.

- Identify what it would take for you to find personal peace.

- Identify how you could become a better peacemaker.

- Brainstorm actions you could take to promote peace in your life, family, and community.

Actions

To find and promote peace, I will:

- Tell my stories about feeling peace.

- Be a peacemaker and bring peace to others by:

- Promote peace in myself, my family, my neighborhood, my state, and the world by:

_____

_____

_____

Remember to use *Make It So!* (Appendix #3) to help you turn your favorite actions into reality.

Beliefs are often more strongly held and less clearly understood than traits or principles. In the next chapter, we'll take a closer look at three beliefs that, for me, have been worth cultivating. As you explore, think about the beliefs you find important and how you might use your stories to convey these beliefs to others.

CHAPTER 5

Three Beliefs Worth Cultivating

"Beliefs are choices. First you choose your beliefs.
Then your beliefs affect your choices."

ROY T BENNETT

Our beliefs shape how we see the world and how we navigate life's challenges and joys. What are the beliefs you hold to be important? Have you ever taken the time to define and ponder them? Some of the most valuable things we can share with children and grandchildren are our personal beliefs—yet these are often overlooked, sometimes because we don't understand them or know how to express them. Here are three areas of belief I cherish:

- God and Spirituality

- Life and The World

- Family

Parents often assume their children share the same beliefs they do but rarely create spaces for open questions and discussions. Similarly, children may have questions about others' beliefs but hesitate to ask. This lack of dialogue can leave important beliefs unexplored. They can't learn from you, and you can't learn from them if there is no discussion. Sharing beliefs provides an opportunity to reflect, connect, and grow together. When sharing, it's essential to encourage curiosity and actively listen to others' perspectives. It is better to explore beliefs together than to try to sell your ideas.

Belief #1: Beliefs About God and Spirituality

"What you are is God's gift to you, what
you become is your gift to God."

HANS URS VON BALTHASAR

The Concept

Have you ever had a moment when you felt something beyond yourself? Maybe a presence, a sense of peace, or an overwhelming touch that you believe is from a supreme being? Our beliefs about God, whatever they may be, are part of our journey. Many people experience God and spirituality in different ways. Our experience may be strong and clear, or vague and amorphous. It may be personal or academic. It probably changes with time, perspective, and experience. It may give us principles to live by or goals we wish to accomplish. It may provide guidance, comfort, forgiveness, direction, or peace. For some, it is a direct and personal relationship. For others, it may be more of a good feeling or hope. The more we can understand our own beliefs about God, the better we can understand ourselves.

Discussing our beliefs about God may be difficult if we haven't really thought it through. And even if we are clear about it, we may not know how to express it. Sharing your stories about your experiences with God or feelings of spirituality can help you define your own beliefs and can help others explore theirs. Consider such questions as:

- How do you experience God?

- What kinds of spiritual experiences have you encountered?

- What have God and religion taught you about life, family, the world, or other people?

- What do God and religion teach you about who you are and your role in the universe?

- What do they teach you about faith, forgiveness, and acceptance?

- How have your beliefs in God shaped your life?

Stories

"I Can't Say That"

As a 19-year-old, I received a call to go on a Church mission to Germany. I was excited. As part of the training, I was to spend three months in the German Language Training Center in Provo, Utah, learning the language.

Each week, the missionaries in the center assembled to bear their testimonies. Many young men would stand and say something like, "I know without a shadow of a doubt that the Church is true." I couldn't honestly say that, so after some uncomfortable weeks, I made an appointment to see the president of the training center to talk about my concerns.

Thinking this might be the end of my mission, I said, "I have been listening to the testimonies other missionaries have borne, saying they knew without any doubts that God lived and the Church was true. I can't say that. I don't know absolutely that all these things are true." I then said, "If absolute knowledge is a requirement, then I probably shouldn't go."

To my surprise, he looked me in the eye and said, "Testimonies come in all forms, and they are constantly changing and clarifying. It is better for you to be honest with yourself."

He then shared a personal experience: "There are times when I know absolutely that things are true, and other times when I hope they are true and depend on the testimony of others. When I have serious questions or doubts about things, I just put them on a shelf in my mind until I am in a personal space where I can ponder them in greater detail." He then encouraged me to stay.

I was grateful for a mission president who was not judgmental and didn't see things as absolute. Over the years, his counsel has stayed with me as my own beliefs have grown.

Questions to Reflect On*: Have you struggled with doubts or questions? What are your stories of struggling with your spiritual beliefs? What are your beliefs?*

_____

_____

_____

Inspiration at the Transfer Board

The Church of Jesus Christ of Latter-day Saints operates hundreds of missions around the world, with transfers occurring every six weeks. That means missionaries are often moved to different locations and given new companions and assignments as needed. This is necessary because there are always new missionaries coming in, others going home, and ongoing needs for new trainers and leaders. In our mission, this was organized on a large wall board with pictures of all the missionaries and the areas where they were assigned.

I arrived as the South Africa Durban Mission President just a week before transfers were scheduled. I had never been to the cities or areas where missionaries were serving and, in fact, had been introduced to very few of them. Fortunately, I had two Assistants to the President who had put together a preliminary transfer approach for me to review.

As I pondered the transfers that night, I felt uneasy about some of the recommendations. So, at two in the morning (not sure why inspiration always seems to come at two in the morning), I went to the office, opened the transfer board, and prayed that I would know what to do. I spent the next few hours moving pictures and assignments around the board.

The next morning, my assistants came in and saw the transfer board had changed and, of course, wanted to know why. I reviewed the changes in assignments and locations I had made, often saying, "I don't really understand the rationale for all the changes I've made, but I know this is how it should be."

As the assistants studied the board, they asked a few questions and finally said, "This is better. It will solve a lot of problems we hadn't addressed." I can't attribute the changes to my own intelligence or intuition. I knew at that time I had been guided by a power far beyond my own.

Questions to Reflect On: *Have you sometimes felt like you were being guided by a higher power? What are your stories of being inspired?*

_____

_____

_____

Leukemia

As a young man, I was out cultivating a sugar beet field when I saw my father's pickup stop at the top of the field. I immediately knew something was wrong when he didn't jump out of the truck. As I reached the top of the field, my worries grew, so I stopped the tractor and went to see what was wrong. Dad motioned for me to get in the truck, and I saw tears in his eyes—something I had never seen before. He had just returned from taking my younger sister to the doctor, where she had been diagnosed with leukemia. At the time, leukemia was thought to be a death sentence. I will never forget the next day, after a family fast, when my father gave my sister a blessing, saying, "Lord, you can have my farm, my health, my life, but please spare the life of my little daughter."

Over the next year, my sister underwent test after test, many of them painful. Finally, Mom and Dad took her to the University of Utah Hospital to see specialists in blood diseases. After even more tests, the doctors told them it wasn't leukemia—but to expect the worst. She had a low white blood cell count, and the part of the cell that fights infection was nearly nonexistent. They said she would probably catch every illness that came along, and with no ability to fight them, she would not be able to survive. They had no treatment, no cure, not even a name for the disease.

In her youth, my sister continued to have many infections and constantly soaked her fingers and toes in salt water, trying to stave off blood poisoning that would begin with even the smallest scratch. Against the doctors' advice, she married and bore three wonderful children. With her exuberant personality, she lives a nonstop life and—perhaps because of her own miracle—spends her time caring for and serving everyone around her: kids, grandkids, neighbors, and friends.

Questions to Reflect On*: Have you experienced any "miracles"? How do you feel about them? What are your stories of unexplainable blessings?*

_____

_____

_____

A Sacred Place in the Seven Devils

One Sunday I was high up in the Seven Devils Mountains with about fifteen Explorer Scouts. We had been camping and hiking, and I asked them to find a place where we could hold a Sunday worship service. Boy, did they find one! It wasn't far from where we were camped but was tucked around some large cliffs and boulders, invisible from the trail. It was like a mini amphitheater sloping down from the cliffs—even with logs and stones for benches. At the bottom was a large square stone that looked like an altar, and beyond the stone was a spectacular view of the valley below.

The boys were reverent as they came into the amphitheater and experienced the view. Soon they started talking, one by one, sharing their beliefs about God. They talked for about an hour, at which point it got really quiet—and I think everyone, including me, expected God to walk around to the altar and talk with us. Maybe he had.

Questions to Reflect On: *When have you felt like you were in the presence of a higher power? What are your stories of having spiritual feelings?*

_____

_____

_____

Key Point

Most of us—whether Christian, Jewish, Muslim, Hindu, Buddhist, or nonbelievers—have had spiritual experiences of one kind or another and hold some concept of a higher power. Often, we don't talk about our feelings or experiences for fear others might laugh, criticize, or simply not understand. I encourage you to think about times in your own life when you have had spiritual experiences and to explore your own beliefs about God and what God means to you. As you identify and tell your own stories, you may find it helps clarify your beliefs. By sharing your stories, you can help children and grandchildren explore and find clarity in their own beliefs.

Possible Activities to Better Clarify and Express Your Beliefs

- Write down your experiences, beliefs, and feelings about God.

- What guidelines for life do you derive from your beliefs?

- What do these guidelines do for you?

- What do you expect from your God?

- What can you do to better understand God?

- What could you read—or who could you talk to—to explore your beliefs and experiences?

- What would you like to change about your relationship with God?

- What could you do to grow spiritually?

Actions

To clarify, better understand, and share my beliefs about God and spirituality, I will:

- Share my stories and experiences.

- More fully develop my understanding of God and spirituality by:

_____

_____

_____

Belief #2: Beliefs About Life and Our World

"The more clearly we can focus our attention on the wonders and realities of the universe about us, the less taste we shall have for destruction."

RACHEL CARSON

The Concept

Have you ever looked up at the night sky and wondered where you fit into it all? Our tiny blue planet orbits the sun, which is only one of millions of suns and solar systems in our Milky Way galaxy, and our galaxy is only one of trillions of galaxies that we know about. This tiny planet, however, is the only one we know of that has evolved to have just the right combination of gases, elements, and temperatures to create and sustain life, and we have evolved to have the brainpower and senses to appreciate and study this rare environment. That raises questions such as:

- How do you view the universe, the Earth, and your place in it?

- What responsibilities do you have to the Earth?

- What responsibilities do you have to other people on the Earth?

- How can you better understand and explore the universe?

- How does understanding the universe make you feel?

- What role do you think people have in this big universe?

Stories

The Impossible Landing

I remember, as a young boy, hearing President Kennedy set the goal of landing a man on the moon before the end of the decade. I, like most of the country, was captivated. It seemed like an impossible task. Incredibly, the country embraced the idea and went to work inventing, developing, building, and testing the means to enact President Kennedy's audacious goal. I followed space developments eagerly: John Glenn's first orbit, every new launch, first flights around the moon. With great excitement, I devoured everything I could find about astronauts and space.

In 1969, I was twenty years old and living in Germany. My missionary companion and I lived in a small apartment without things such as a television, bath, or shower—we would go weekly to the city baths. We knew the United States was attempting to land a man on the moon soon, but didn't really have the means to follow what was happening on a regular basis.

Fortunately, while walking home from our work area one evening, we passed an appliance store, and there, through the display window, we could see a small black-and-white television just as it was showing Neil Armstrong stepping onto the surface of the moon.

We stood on the sidewalk watching and cheering as he said, "That's one small step for man, one giant leap for mankind." I remember having a rush of feelings: I was proud to be an American. I was in awe of the human achievement, and I worried whether the astronauts would be able to return safely.

That was also when I began to realize that not only was our understanding of the universe exploding, but—with all the new technology—the world I was living in was about to change dramatically. And this was before cell phones, home computers, the internet, and social media came to be. It was humbling to wonder what all this new invention and information would bring.

Questions to Reflect On: *What are your thoughts on our expanding knowledge of the universe? What are your feelings about the changes brought about by technological advances? What are your personal stories of experiencing the universe?*

_____

_____

_____

A Realization From the Southern Sky

When we first moved to Harare, Zimbabwe, we lived outside the city in a secluded area. Harare sits at almost 5,000 feet, with clear air and very little light pollution. The night sky was brilliant. I will never forget walking out into the backyard—probably the day after we moved in—and seeing, for the first time, the southern sky, gazing at the Southern Cross and marveling at a whole array of new stars and constellations. Since then, I have been fascinated as pictures from the Hubble and Webb space telescopes have vastly expanded our understanding of the universe. I continue to be amazed by our universe and our role in it.

In the past, we didn't think much about our little blue planet. It was just there and seemed to take care of itself. We thought resources were unlimited—that we could use them without much thought. We did not realize just how fragile this planet is. Over time, the results of indiscriminate pollution, unintended consequences, and, more recently, global warming have become increasingly obvious and threatening.

Today's issues are no longer just community- or nation-based. Across the globe, our systems of production—for goods, energy, and food— have become interdependent. Our risks from the misuse of resources, pollution, and now global warming have also become interdependent. The planet is increasingly at risk, but how do you get eight billion people, in hundreds of countries, competing for the same resources, to agree on a way forward?

The good news is that we are trying, and there is a growing realization that, to save ourselves, we will have to manage our shared resources with greater care and respect.

Questions to Reflect On: *What are your thoughts as you view the night sky? What are your thoughts on your personal responsibility for our planet? What stories can you tell of helping to care for the planet?*

_____

_____

_____

Picking Up Trash While Camping

One summer, I was camping with some of our kids up on Jughandle Mountain, just south of McCall, Idaho. It was a beautiful spot, high in the mountains, by a crystal-clear lake. It was just an overnight camp, but as we packed up to leave the next morning, we picked up every bit of scrap from around our campsite and then, with plastic bags, went around to abandoned neighboring campsites and picked up their trash.

The kids gave me a little pushback about cleaning up the other camps, saying, "Why should we have to clean that up? We didn't make that mess!" This gave me the opportunity to talk about stewardship and responsibility to the planet. I always made it a point, when we traveled, to try to leave things better than we found them, and I think the kids have learned to follow the same habits. They got this stewardship concept at home too, where my wife is an avid recycler and tries to change our behaviors whenever she reads about something that might be harming the environment.

Questions to Reflect On: *What are your views on pollution, environmentalism, recycling, and wind and solar power? How do you view your responsibility? What are your stories of understanding and caring for the planet?*

_____

_____

_____

Polaroids in Rwanda

The road from Rwanda to Uganda passes through towering volcanic mountains. They are heavily forested and, being on the equator and nourished by the rich volcanic soil, are a brilliant green.

We were searching for an orphanage I wanted to visit, and after a few wrong turns, we managed to find it nestled in the mountains. The facility was overcrowded; the outside walls were riddled with bullet holes from ongoing skirmishes. But it was clean and well organized— especially given the lack of resources. They seldom had visitors, and many of the kids had never seen a white guy before and were curious.

Family watching a poloroid develop in mountains of Uganda

I grouped some of them together and took a picture with my Polaroid. I was kneeling on the ground so they could watch. When the picture came out of the camera, it was gray and not yet developed. The kids were confused. As the film developed, the confusion quickly turned to excitement, and I was soon nearly suffocated by crowds of kids trying to watch the image appear and see themselves for the very first time.

I could not help but think that, although this was their world as much as mine, and they were no different than kids anywhere else in the world, their lack of opportunity gave them a very different view of life, the planet, and the universe.

Questions to Reflect On: *What do you think about the differences in resources and opportunity around the world? What are your stories of interacting with other cultures?*

_____

_____

_____

Only One Galaxy

I recently saw a news article noting that it's been 100 years since the discovery that there are galaxies beyond our own. That's just 25 years before I was born. Reading this article made me reflect on how far we humans have come since that discovery. The latest news I saw estimated that there are at least three trillion galaxies, each with millions of solar-type systems. Understanding that we are just a tiny piece of the larger universe doesn't make me feel small—it makes me feel inspired to contribute, in my own way, to the collective pursuit of knowledge.

This geometric explosion of knowledge has occurred in nearly every area of science—all brought about by curious and dedicated people dreaming dreams and working together to explore, invent, discover, and build. I consider myself lucky to be part of such an extraordinary world in such an extraordinary time.

Questions to Reflect On: *How do you view your role in the galaxy? What recent discoveries have changed your view of life? What are your stories of finding a place in the world?*

_____

_____

_____

Key Point

We are all part of one vast universe, a fascinating solar system, and a life-giving planet. Since there are many of us, we sometimes unwittingly damage the world we live in—and the people in it. As fragile as life is, we each have a responsibility to understand it, preserve it, and make it better for ourselves and for everyone else.

Possible Activities

- Write down your thoughts on environmentalism—clean air, clean water, safe food, and sustainability.

- Write down your thoughts about issues such as global warming, recycling, plastic pollution, and wind power.

- What could you do to better understand our planet and environmentalism?

- List ways you could be a better steward.

- Visit a planetarium or a landfill.

- Check out one of your local rivers or lakes.

Actions

- I will share personal stories that have shaped my concept of the universe and its meaning.

- To more fully understand the universe and become a better steward, I will:

_____

_____

_____

Belief #3: Beliefs About Family

"The bond that links your true family is not one of blood, but of respect and joy in each other's life."

RICHARD BACH

The Concept

What does family mean to you? Is it the people you grew up with, the ones who raised you, or those you've chosen along the way? Some are more traditional, some are blended, and some are put together out of necessity. Some are small and immediate, while others are extended, with grandparents, great-grandparents, aunts, and uncles. Sometimes family includes the whole neighborhood.

These families, however defined, are where we grow up and are hopefully taught, loved, and supported unconditionally. They provide food, shelter, and protection, but they also give us a sense of belonging, identity, and worth. They are the basic organization of humankind.

Family traditions and values can strengthen bonds and provide future generations with a blueprint for navigating life.

Stories

A Sandwich in the Bathtub

I was incredibly fortunate to have had great parents. I never saw them fight and always knew they loved each other and me. My dad was a hardworking farmer, and while neither Mom nor Dad had the opportunity for a college education, in our house education was paramount. Going to college wasn't really a decision; it was just what came after high school. They made sure we had the best opportunities.

They modeled concepts of honesty, hard work, and love. They were respected and active in the community. I have memories of my dad coming in from work and my mom feeding him a sandwich while he was in the bathtub so he could clean up and head off to a church or school board meeting. Oh, we had our challenges, disagreements, and minor rebellions—just like all families. I was one who would argue about everything. But working through those disagreements is part of what makes strong families.

I grew up thinking everyone's family life was like mine. Only later did I discover how sheltered and fortunate my upbringing had been.

Questions to Reflect On: *Who is your family? How has your family shaped you? What are your cherished stories of family life?*

Marrying My Best Friend

Susan and I were introduced to each other by my business partner. Like many couples in the San Francisco Bay Area, we spent time in our courtship hiking, going to shows and concerts, eating, traveling, and talking. We became best friends. She told me early on that I had a reputation for "love them and leave them" and made me promise that if I ever wanted to leave the relationship, I would tell her in person and not just disappear. Forty-five years and six children later, I haven't yet gathered the courage to tell her. *Just kidding!*

My proposal was not exactly the most romantic. After a hike, I went over to her apartment, still in my dirty clothes, knocked on her door, and said, "I just don't think this relationship is working very well." I think she was terrified. I then said, "I think it would be better if we just got married." She said, "Stay right there!" and disappeared. As it turned out, she was trying to call friends and relatives to tell them I had proposed, thinking that if it were public, I couldn't back out. Unfortunately for her, she couldn't reach anyone, but she said, "Yes" anyway. I think marrying your best friend is a great idea. Our relationship is still built on being able to talk about everything.

Questions to Reflect On: *What are your most important relationships? How have your relationships developed? What stories can you share about your important relationships?*

_____

_____

_____

Teaching Grandkids to Sail

Not long ago, I was able to go with three of my grandchildren and their parents to Belize so I could teach them to sail. What a wonderful opportunity for a grandfather! I sent them written sailing lessons so they could prepare for the trip and even made graduation certificates for completing Grandpa's Sailing Course. We had a ball.

They got to see porpoises, giant sea turtles, manatees, rays, sharks, and all kinds of fish and coral. They learned to set and trim the sails, come about, and anchor. They learned to steer a straight course, the basics of navigation, and, of course, we told lots of stories. Currently, I am teaching my grandchildren in Utah how to rappel. There is a saying in my church that "Families are Forever." Sometimes, we joke that the statement is more of a curse than a promise, but it really is true. Families are the glue that holds societies together.

Questions to Reflect On: *How do you describe families? What values or traditions have been most meaningful in your family? What are your stories about family life?*

_____

_____

_____

Two Babies on a Plane

(Warning: This story is a little longer, but I think you will find it interesting.)

When Susan and I got married, we talked about having a mixed-race family; life then interfered. We got busy with work, school, and raising a family, and the subject didn't come back up. Thirteen years later, we had moved to Idaho with our four kids and thought our family was complete. *Au contraire!* There was a family in our neighborhood—the

Tolleys—with kids of varying ethnic backgrounds, and Susan came home one day and said, "Remember us talking about having a mixed-race family?" I said, "Yes," and she said, "Well, are you still interested?" I was 44 at the time, and our youngest was already five, but I said, "Sure, let's do it." All our friends thought we were crazy, but we started the process for adoption.

The adoption process is fairly rigorous. You get police and background checks, submit income statements, and basically must prove that you are able to safely support the children you adopt. We learned first that we were too old for Asian adoptions and that younger parents were at the front of the line for U.S. adoptions. Our adoption counselor then said, "Would you consider adopting a Black baby?" We said, "We would love to." We didn't care what race the children were. Our view was that babies, no matter their color or ethnicity, just need parents who will love them.

We always felt we would be adopting two babies and even asked about two young siblings or twins. The answer was, "No, you have to do one adoption, wait a year to finalize, then start the whole process over." Undeterred, we went out and bought a double stroller and two cribs.

Our Family Profile had been sent out to three different agencies, including one in Washington, D.C., and one in Atlanta. Our counselor said the Atlanta agency probably wouldn't consider us eligible because they were a Christian agency and didn't consider The Church of Jesus Christ of Latter-day Saints as being Christian. I said to Susan, "I bet we get a baby from there."

Just a few weeks after sending out our paperwork, we got a call from the agency in Washington, D.C., saying they had a baby for us. Two days later, the agency in Atlanta called with another baby. We wanted to get both, but the agency, again, said, "No." Now we had three agencies involved: Boise, Atlanta, and Washington. After what seemed like dozens of calls, all three agencies miraculously agreed to let us go ahead with the double adoption.

The legal requirements had to be completed, but just three weeks later, Susan hopped on a plane and went to Washington, D.C., to pick up Jeffrey, and one week later, I caught a plane to Atlanta to pick up Hunter.

Our newest family members

I discovered there aren't many middle-aged white men in airports with Black babies. I learned something interesting about that. Black people would come up to look at the baby and start talking to me. White people, I could tell, were interested but wouldn't come speak to me.

As it turned out, the boys were born on the very same day, about four hours apart. As of this writing, they are now thirty-two, graduated from college, and gainfully employed. They also had the experience of living many years in Africa while I was doing humanitarian work.

Susan and I, along with all the kids, feel just as connected as if we were all blood relations, regardless of color and birth details. We have all been enriched by being a mixed-race family.

Questions to Reflect On: What do you think about adoption? What do you think about multiracial adoption? What stories have shaped your beliefs about families?

_____

_____

_____

Key Point

For most of us, families are the focal point of our lives—whether those are the families we grew up in, the ones we now have, or the ones we are trying to create. Whether our family is traditional or nontraditional, it is where we learn, love, value, and trust. We all have the responsibility to help our families be the best they can be.

Possible Activities

- Reach out to a family member with whom you might be out of contact.

- Repair a family relationship.

- Do something with a family member where you can learn and explore.

- Have younger folks draw a picture of their family and talk about it.

- Tell stories and teach principles to family members.

- Create a common family motto or symbol.

- Find a way to spend more time together.

- Do something to create a family memory.

Actions

- I will share my stories about my family.

- To strengthen my family, I will:

_____

_____

_____

Remember to use *"Make It So!"* (Appendix #3) to help you turn your favorite actions into reality.

Traits, principles, and beliefs give us direction, but they truly come to life when we share them with others. They are the bridges that connect our values and experiences to the people we care most about. In the next chapter, we will explore how to strengthen and maintain your newfound skills of storytelling and discussion.

CHAPTER 6

Moving On

*"I just got to keep going and keep building on my
game and get better and better each season."*

Justin Jefferson

At this point, you have read a lot of stories, pondered many Traits, Principles, and Beliefs, and, hopefully, clarified many of your own values while starting to tell your own stories. In your notes you have compiled quite a list of stories you could tell and beliefs, traits and principles you value. Most importantly, you have been engaging with your kids and grandkids in fun and meaningful conversations.

Storytelling and discussing important issues aren't just one-time events; they are an ongoing process that evolves as you, your children, and your grandchildren age and gain experience. As long as we continue sharing, listening, and reflecting, the power of storytelling grows, and our ability to share values and engage in meaningful conversation deepens.

Here are some ways to take what you've learned so far and turn it into a lasting practice.

Create New Traditions

Storytelling and open discussion can become a cherished tradition in your family. Whether it's a regular gathering, a special event, or a quiet moment before bedtime, find ways to make stories a part of your life. Consider:

- **Pondering, Clarifying, and Writing Down**: Identify the traits and beliefs that have shaped your life, and find the stories that illustrate these beliefs that you would like to pass on. Your notes can be a great resource for this activity.

- **Holding Family Story Nights**: Pick a night each week or maybe each month for everyone to share a story. You could set a theme—like "A Time I Felt Brave" or "A Favorite Childhood Memory"—or just let the stories flow naturally. It may or may not turn into a discussion of a specific trait or belief.

- **Creating a Story Calendar:** Write down a story for each day or week. Use a calendar or journal to keep track of the stories you've told and the ones you want to share next.

- **Creating a Topic Calendar:** Write down the important topics you've discussed and things you would like to discuss or revisit in the future.

- **Starting a Family Newsletter:** This could be monthly or even quarterly to get started. Have everyone, no matter where they live, contribute stories that have shaped their lives, put them together, and send them out. It's a great way to learn and share, especially for families separated by geography.

- **Recording the Stories:** Use your phone, camera, or even a pen to record the stories. These can become treasured keepsakes, especially when you record some of the wisdom of children.

- **Listening and Learning:** Storytelling isn't just about talking; it's also about listening. The more you listen, the more you'll discover about the people around you. Ask questions about what topics interest them. Ask for more details in their stories. Ask what they heard or learned from a story or discussion.

- **Including Everyone:** Once you have told a story, ask others to share their own. This will create some of the most memorable events. Once they get used to it, people—especially children—love to share their own stories.

- **Honoring All Stories:** Not every story will be lighthearted or have a happy ending. Be open to hearing stories about struggles, challenges, and lessons learned.

- **Being Fully Present:** Put away distractions and give your full attention when someone shares a story. Show interest through eye contact, nodding, and asking follow-up questions. Taking a call, sending a text, or checking social media while someone else is telling their story is a sure way to kill the moment.

Incorporate Technology

Today's digital world gives us new ways to help preserve and share stories that were once unimaginable. Consider using:

- **Video Recordings**: Record yourself or your loved ones telling stories. These videos can be shared with faraway family members or archived for future generations. My closest grandchildren live four hours away, but our daughter-in-law sends regular video clips of things they are doing, and we talk to them often on Zoom. Even the two-year-olds want to be part of the discussion, and the chats often turn into a performance or discussion.

- **Social Media and Blogs**: Share your stories online to reach a wider audience. During our time in Africa, my wife kept a blog of our activities, and it is still shared and treasured by many of those who worked with us.

- **Story Apps:** Explore apps that can help you capture and organize stories. Some even allow you to add photos, videos, and audio for a multimedia experience.

- **Zoom**: Use Zoom or similar apps to connect with family and friends who are far away. These apps are getting easier to use, and it is amazing when you have video to go with the audio. Seeing and interacting with each other live makes all the difference.

- **Electronic Picture Frames:** We have an electronic picture frame in our kitchen that shows pictures of kids, grandkids, and events at different times in their lives. Thousands of pictures rotate through it. It is hard to pass by without stopping for a look, which often sparks questions: "Who is that? What is that? Where was this? When was this?" Sometimes we find groups of grandchildren or adults standing in front of the frame, mesmerized.

- **Explore Family History Websites:** FamilySearch, Ancestry, MyHeritage and many others can aid you in recording and saving your stories.

Tip: Remember to use the stories, pictures, videos, and written histories after you record them. Sometimes we record events and then store them away where no one will ever see or hear them, causing the wisdom to get lost.

Keep Reflecting

Your understanding of your own values and beliefs may grow and change over time. Reflecting on your stories can deepen your insights and help you see connections you hadn't noticed before. Consider:

- **Adapting Your stories:** As you experience more of life, you constantly evolve, and so do your children and grandchildren. A topic you discuss briefly when they are seven could become a very different discussion when they are fifteen.

- **Journaling**: Write down your thoughts, memories, and reflections regularly. Over time, these entries may reveal patterns and themes in your life and will certainly spark additional stories.

- **Morning Meditations**: Have a quiet time each day reflecting on a story or value that matters to you. It is a great way to clarify your own thinking and bring long-forgotten stories to mind. (See Appendix #1 for tips on meditation.)

Write Your Own Book

You may have felt you didn't have the skills or had nothing to say, but hopefully storytelling has changed that. Learning to tell stories makes it easier for you to start.

- You could write a book, something like this one, where you use your stories to tell about the traits, principles, and beliefs you cherish. Just going through this book you have the beginnings of your own book of wisdom.

- You could preserve your own life history by telling stories about each period of your life.

Like so many things we have discussed, the hardest part of writing a book is getting started. To begin, all you need to do is start writing down your own stories; organizing them can come later. You might decide you want to publish the book, or maybe you just want to make it available to your children and grandchildren.

Possible Activities

- Go to the website steve-mann.com (Appendix #4) to find additional information and resources.

- Review all the Actions you wrote down that you wanted to try and all the principles, traits and beliefs you want to develop. Identify the ones most important to you, then use the *"Make It So!"* Planning Sheets found on the website to turn that planned action into reality.

- Help someone else—an elderly friend, your grandparents, or a family member who may be a little disconnected—reconnect with and tell their stories.

- What other activities or tools can you think of to help storytelling become a habit?

Actions

To keep improving my own storytelling and ability to talk productively with children and grandchildren, I will:

_____

_____

_____

A Final Word

Undoubtedly, you have noticed the underlying sense of confidence and optimism in my stories and key points. I hope this has been contagious and has inspired you, your children, and your grandchildren. Maybe sometime in the future, your stories—and this sense of optimism—will empower a struggling great-grandchild or some other young man or woman who comes across your stories to find greater joy, understanding, purpose, and a sense of belonging in their lives.

Thank you for taking this journey with me. Your willingness to reflect, share, and grow is a gift not just to yourself but to everyone whose life you touch. The stories and values you carry have the power to inspire, connect, and create hope. So, keep moving. Keep sharing. Keep building bridges through the power of storytelling and meaningful conversations.

The best chapters of this journey are still ahead.

Bonus Chapter: Discussing Controversial Issues

Now it's time to download the bonus chapter, where you'll discover how to once again talk with friends and family about important—but sometimes contentious—issues.

In our polarized age, neighbors often don't talk to neighbors. Family members avoid one another. When we do talk, it's about sports or the weather, what's for dinner, or what movies are streaming. We seem to avoid sensitive or potentially controversial topics almost to an extreme. Isn't it sad that we can no longer learn about—or share—the things in life that truly matter?

In Chapter 7, you'll learn how to apply what you've discovered so far to conversations with friends and family about difficult topics. You'll learn how to reopen channels of communication that once formed the bedrock of our relationships. And you'll see how you can help rebuild the avenues of discussion so essential to our democracy.

Download Chapter 7 (How to Talk With Friends and Family About Controversial Issues) now by going to the website steve-mann.com.

APPENDIX

#1. Morning Meditations

Over the years, I've discovered the power of starting each day with quiet reflection. I usually do some deep breathing exercises, then sit on my mat and ponder for a while. Weather permitting, I do this outside as the sun comes up, and I can feel the warmth of its rays on my face. I usually contemplate, meditate, or ponder on:

1.   Things I am grateful for

2.   Things that bring me joy

3.   Things I love

4.   Peace

You can meditate on anything you want. Sometimes I contemplate an experience or discussion I have had, a new learning, a person I am trying to better understand, an issue I may be grappling with, something I have learned from reading, or the news. Sometimes I ponder one of the traits, beliefs, or principles and what I might do to better understand and act on it.

You don't need to be a meditation expert to benefit from this practice. The goal isn't perfection; it's simply to create a calm, intentional space to start the day. Sometimes my meditations turn into prayer. Sometimes

I get new inspirations, and sometimes I just find a little peace before the start of the day.

To give you an idea of what this is like, here are some of the things that come to mind when I contemplate in my four basic areas:

I am grateful for:

The world I live in: The weather, geography, colors, flora and fauna, and seasons. The mountains, savannas, deserts, rivers, oceans, and rainbows. The night and day, and heat, cold, rain, and snow, and especially the warmth of the sun. (I think I could easily have joined the ancient Egyptians in worshiping the sun.) The roadrunners and quail scurrying around my yard, and the hawks and eagles overhead. The lizards speeding away as our desert tortoises lumber out in the mornings for their breakfast.

The universe I am part of: The trillions of galaxies, hundreds of trillions of solar systems, black holes, and comets. When I was a kid, we didn't know most of this stuff was out there, so I am grateful for the scientists and instruments helping us better understand and appreciate this incredible space we call home.

My body: And all the little parts that make it work, including the artificial ones like shoulders, hips, pacemakers, and now hearing aids. I'm grateful, too, for the scientists, doctors, and engineers who invent and build these incredible parts that allow me to keep going.

Eyes that let me see sunrises, sunsets, rainbows, blue skies, and the moon and stars at night. They also guide me, keep me from danger, and let me experience Van Gogh's *Starry Night.*

Ears that let me hear songbirds tweeting and crows cawing in the morning, the thunder and crack of lightning in a thunderstorm, and the beauty of a sonata. They alert me to trouble and herald the arrival of friends and family.

A tongue that lets me taste ice cream and grilled salmon, and alerts me when things might be poisonous.

A nose that not only helps me breathe and be wary of dirty diapers, but also detects the smell of fresh pizza and newly mown hay.

Skin that protects all my body parts, miraculously heals itself, and tells me of various textures. It warns me of hot and cold, sharp objects, and lets me feel the soft skin of a newborn.

Arms, legs, hands and feet that help me move around, grab things, keep me out of harm's way, and lead me into exploration.

Systems such as the nervous, vascular, muscular, and lymphatic systems—but I think you get the idea. We all have these incredible bodies that let us experience the world.

Health and energy that allow me to enjoy life and continue making a contribution.

A brain that manages all these parts, translates all this input into awe and appreciation, and keeps me safe, entertained, and hopeful. I find the simple things my body does amazing. For instance, isn't it amazing that my brain can think that my little toe should move, and it does?

People: I have had the opportunity to see much of the world and interact with all kinds of people. I am grateful for all the different cultures, colors, ethnicities, and religions that make up this family of humankind. I'm grateful for their differences, but also their sameness. They all just want to keep their children and communities safe and enjoy the world, just as I do.

Susan, my wife of 46 years, who has supported and encouraged me and gone along with all my crazy ideas as she raised our children—often with me absent.

Kids and grandkids. I think they are more fun now than when they were little. While it is hard to watch them struggle with life's challenges, it is exciting to see them embrace life and find ways to contribute.

Friends. I have developed many great friendships at work, while building foundations, and in all the places we have lived.

Daily life. All the little things—clean air and water, food, friendships, new thoughts, new activities, being able to go for walks and say hi to neighbors, a kiss from my wife, a call from my kids and grandkids.

What are you grateful for?

I find joy in:

- All the things I am grateful for.

- Being able to build and create—whether it's a company, a foundation, a family, or even a Lego set.

- Contributing and making a positive difference in people's lives.

- Being with my family.

- Being outside—whether on a sailboat, hanging on a rope from a piece of granite high up on a mountain, or exploring the red rock around St. George, Utah.

- Sports like sailing, climbing, hiking, and skiing.

- My friends and neighbors.

- Being able to think and reason.

- Being able to make a contribution.

- The teachings of Jesus Christ: love, forgiveness, service, acceptance, and being slow to judge.

- Just being.

What brings you joy?

I love:

- The phrase from the Declaration of Independence: *"We hold these truths to be self-evident, that all men are created equal, that they are endowed by their Creator with certain unalienable Rights, that among these are Life, Liberty and the pursuit of Happiness."*

- The French version: *Liberty, Equality, Fraternity*

- The brilliance of our Founding Fathers.

- My wife and family.

- My faith and testimony.

- Just being, feeling, and thinking.

What—or who—do you love?

I experience peace:

- From peacemakers trying to make things better.

- From those who work toward resolution.

- In the quiet of being alone in the wilderness.

- With the wind in my face, setting the sails on a perfect sea.

- In the silence of the night, looking out at a full moon.

- In seeing the end of a war or hostilities anywhere in the world.

- From a civil discussion.

- When my beliefs and my actions are congruent.

- By just clearing my mind.

What brings you peace?

It seems that no matter how often I do these meditations, I come up with new things to be grateful for and amazed by.

#2. Talk on Equality

As I was writing this book, I came across a long-forgotten talk I had given on the steps of the Idaho State Capitol not long after we adopted our two youngest sons. I believe it was at the conclusion of a march for equality. Nearly forty years later, it still reflects my views. It might serve as a good starting point for discussion as you explore the topic of equality with others.

Welcome, brothers and sisters. Welcome to the steps of the Capitol on this cold, damp winter night. There are some fathers in the audience, and I would like to address my remarks to you, as fathers, for just a moment.

I think all of us, as fathers, find it hard when our kids go out into the world for the first time. You know—that first night away from home, that first day at school, that first driver's license.

But for me, like for many of you, that fear is a little different. You see, two of my children are a different color. Two of my children are Black. And I, as a father—like many of you—have to send them out into the world knowing there are people who want to kill them just because of their color.

I don't know what causes that kind of hate. I suppose it is part fear and many parts ignorance. But I do know that we, as a community—as a society—cannot tolerate it.

We have been, we are, and we will continue to be a multiethnic, multiracial, and multi religious society. For over 250 years, we have drawn our strength from this diversity. Now is not the time to turn back.

The price we pay for fear, ignorance, and prejudice is the price of a holocaust—or the kind of wholesale slaughter we see in Rwanda today. Turning back now would cost us our soul, our nationhood, and our future. And that cost is too high.

We are all Americans. We are all brothers and sisters. And we must find a way—together—to draw strength and unity from our similarities, and to celebrate and rejoice in our differences.

You have all heard the story of how the mighty Mississippi starts with a trickle of snowmelt high in Yellowstone. Hate begins the same way— with little fears, little slurs, little but untrue beliefs, and small acts of separation.

As important as they are, it is not the laws from Washington that will make the difference in our relationships. It is the effort each of us makes to reach out, to stop prejudice, to speak instead of remaining silent, that will truly make the difference.

How many of us—even those of us here on the Capitol steps tonight— have diverted our eyes or looked down when passing someone of a different color or ethnic background? Is it because of fear, uncertainty, or embarrassment? I don't know. But this is where the greater violence begins.

I am not asking for us all to march on Washington. I am simply asking that, instead of turning away, we look that person in the eye, smile, and say hello. If we can all take just this little step, go out of our way just this one little bit, the violence will stop.

Why? Because with this simple act of acknowledgment, we begin the discovery that we are all just ordinary people, regardless of our color. We all have the same fears, the same loves and sorrows, the same hopes for the future, and the same families and friends we care about.

#3. Make It So!

In the course of reading and exploring each chapter, you have written down actions or activities you would like to pursue to learn more and help you better acquire a trait or ability.

You can use the following "*Make It So!*" Planning Sheets, to outline each of the activities you want to complete and your plans for completing them. The six steps outlined below can help you develop an achievable plan. Additional "*Make It So!*" Planning Sheets can be found at steve-mann.com

1. Review all the actions you wrote down under Traits, Principles, Beliefs, and Talking with Friends. Select the key actions you most want to explore, then write each one down on a "*Make It So!*" Planning Sheet like the one below.

2. Write a brief description of why you want to complete this activity and the result you expect from it.

3. Write down 3–4 steps you need to take to complete each action, including the first thing you want to do to get started.

4. Write down the roadblocks you think will get in the way of achieving your goals and, most importantly, how you will overcome them (solutions).

5. Identify someone who you think could help you achieve your goals, then share your goals with them. Ask them to check up with you periodically to see how you are doing.

6. Now just do it. *"Make it So!"*

As you complete each activity you might want to just sign it and put it where you can keep track of your progress

Please feel free to copy the planning sheet or download more from the website:
steve-mann.com

"Make It So!" Planning Sheet

Step 1 *Planned Action:*

_____

_____

_____

_____

Step 2 *Expected Outcome:*

_____

_____

_____

Step 3 *Key Steps to Complete Planned Action:*

_____

_____

_____

_____

Step 4 *Roadblocks and Solutions:*

_____

_____

_____

_____

Step 5 *Who can help you, their contact information, and the date you will contact them:*

_____

_____

_____

_____

#4. Website Contact and Content

Interested readers can find additional content by going to steve-mann.com. Here is some of what you will find:

Download: Bonus Chapter 7 (PDF or audio)

Learn about: The book, the author.

Contact the author: To schedule podcasts or speaking engagements.

Download: Additional "***Make It So!***" Planning Sheets.

Bonus Story: Just for fun!

Acknowledgements

First, my heartfelt thanks to my wife, Susan, for her encouragement, suggestions, corrections, and edits—and more importantly, for putting up with my craziness, boom revelations, and constant change all these years. Her love is what made the stories, the experiences, and this book possible.

I would also like to thank our children for managing all the changes my life has caused in theirs—with grace. While things were sometimes difficult, I believe they look back on most of their experiences fondly. A special thanks to our grandchildren, whose asking for stories instigated this whole adventure.

Special thanks to my son Jeffrey for his guidance, patience, skill and hard work in getting the book published, building me a social media presence, and for his marketing expertise in letting the world know the book exists.

Thanks to my son Parker for editing the pictures, converting from color to black & white, and preparing them for publication.

Thanks as well to all of the *editors, designers, publishers, marketers, coaches* as SelfPublishing who corrected, cajoled, and encouraged.

Finally, I would like to thank you, the reader, for putting up with my irrational enthusiasm. I know such optimism can be irritating for some—but it's just the way I am.

Photo Credits

- Photos 10, 12, and 13 are in the public domain and have been modified for publication.

- Photo 16: Traditional Kalanga meal preparation (modified from original), 2017. Photo provided by Mompati Dikunwane via Wikimedia Commons. Licensed under CC BY-SA 4.0: https://creativecommons.org/licenses/by-sa/4.0/.

- All other photos are courtesy of the author.

Printed in Dunstable, United Kingdom

70461314R00107